Heart Over Heels

By the same author:

OPEN HEART THERAPY

TWO HEARTS ARE BETTER THAN ONE

BIRTH & RELATIONSHIPS
(co-authored with Sondra Ray)

Heart Over Heels

50 WAYS *NOT* TO LOSE YOUR LOVER

Bob Mandel

CELESTIAL ARTS
Berkeley, California

CELESTIAL ARTS
P.O. Box 7327
Berkeley, California 94707

Cover design by Ken Scott
Text design by Nancy Austin
Composition by Wilsted & Taylor, Oakland

Library of Congress Cataloging-in-Publication Data

Mandel, Robert Steven, 1943–
    Heart over heels: 50 ways not to lose your lover / Bob Mandel.
        p.   cm.
    ISBN 0-89087-541-3
    1. Love.   2. Interpersonal relations.   I. Title
HQ801.M368   1989   88-31159
646.7'8—dc19   CIP

Manufactured in the United States of America

First Printing, 1989

0   9   8   7   6   5   4   3   2   1

INTRODUCTION

This is a hypothetical case study, the story of an imaginary relationship, the path and process two unique individuals might share on a journey towards being together forever. It is a story beginning in the 1960s, reaching back into the 1940s and stretching forward into the twenty-first century.

This book evolved in its own organic way. When I teach The Loving Relationships Training (LRT), I draw two stick figures on a blackboard every Saturday morning. I use these two figures, which I call George and Martha, as examples of the ways in which unconscious patterning can affect intimate relationships in the course of their growth. Over the last ten years these stick figures have become very real characters in my mind, and I often find myself elaborating their story in great detail, as though they were friends of mine I had known for a very long time. In a way this is the story of two characters that "got away," i.e., they sprung forth from my imagination and claimed a life of their own, which I could only witness. Whereas I began by using them as instruments of teaching, they finally became my teachers, guides and fellow spiritual travelers. I dedicate this book to them, George & Martha.

The fifty chapters of this book are, first of all, fifty phases of George and Martha's relationship. They are, secondly, fifty ways not to lose your lover, fifty lessons that, when mastered, will assist you in leaving your leaving pattern (or pattern of abandonment) and evolving a healthy staying pattern. Some of these lessons are obvious, others are more subtle.

Some are mundane, others magical. When you combine common sense with a sense of the miraculous, you master the fifty ways.

Thirdly, this is a book of affirmations. Each chapter is complete with twenty affirmations that illustrate the particular lesson, or way, in question. An affirmation is a simple positive thought on which you focus your attention in order to see a situation in a new, positive light. Since your thoughts are creative, the more you choose to change your mind, the more you are, in fact, choosing to change your experience. I suggest you create a cassette tape in your own voice, repeating each affirmation twice, and listen to the tape while meditating, rebirthing or just relaxing. If there is any affirmation to which you have strong resistance, you should write it out twenty times a day, drawing a vertical line down the middle of the page and using the right hand side as your response column, where you record and release any negative thoughts in opposition to the positive one.

You can read this book on any of three levels then—as an entertaining story, as fifty essays on how not to lose your lover, or as a thousand affirmations to support the longevity of your loving relationships.

However your read it, may it prove beneficial to the health and eternality of your love life. You deserve miracles. If not you, who?

The Fifty Ways

Heart Over Heels

—1—

Seeing with Your Eyes Closed

Martha closed her eyes and spread her legs. As Philip entered her, she sighed deeply and drifted off.

She was bored with sex, bored with Philip, bored with herself, bored with life. So as she continued to go through the motions of a relationship, sleepwalking through her life, she found herself drifting more and more, a sinking, unfulfilled feeling pulling her off into the distance.

She was thinking about the relationships symposium coming up, about the assignment to write a vision of her love life of the future. As Philip poured more and more of himself into her, she struggled to think of her ideal lover and how his touch might feel.

She was confused by the whole assignment. In her mind you didn't make up a vision, they just sort of happened to you. Or to some folk. And they were called visionaries. And maybe what they saw was true and maybe it wasn't. The topic of visions made her nervous.

Philip was breathing hard and fast. "I love you," he whispered.

Was she supposed to see her future, actually travel in time, take a mental polaroid, then come back and write it down on paper? Or was she just supposed to imagine it, make it up, and, if so, why? What good would it do her?

She could only relate it to painting. Whenever she felt a painting call her, she would close her eyes and let it come to her. She could see the whole thing, more real than reality, every single detail, color, shade,

1

shape, figure. Then she'd open her eyes, forget what she saw and start painting. Usually the finished product came out a lot like her mind's picture. Whether that meant she had actually seen the painting before painting it or had a picture in her mind which she then created, she did not know. She did know that whenever she closed her eyes to look, she felt lightheaded, separate from her body, and someplace else entirely.

"Don't move, baby, don't move."

She took a deep breath, hopelessly removed from Philip, and, letting the air out slowly, felt a little dizzy, started to black out, then, suddenly, she saw the whole thing. She was there. In the painting. In her future. And watching it at the same time. It was a curious picture, like a medieval church painting, the life of a saint, only futuristic at the same time.

"I'm coming, I'm coming."

In the foreground was a beach with dolphins dancing in the sea. A cliff rose up to a ridge where a beautiful Mediterranean villa stood, Spanish-style architecture with sweeping verandas, courtyards, and plenty of light. On the terrace, facing a sun setting into the sea, she stood with her ideal mate, their eyes radiating light and gazing at the center of the scene. Here was a twisted olive tree, ripe with fruit, and a golden cherub on a limb, playing his harp, while two doves danced in midair. The colors were mostly pastels. The painting had many levels, layers, scenes and stories. The feeling was one of perfect love.

"That was great." Philip rolled over on his back, oblivious to the tears in Martha's eyes. She knew he would be gone in the morning. It was all over.

Or was it just beginning?

George was preparing to leave yet another brief relationship. Laura, the latest in a long line of voluptuous victims, was lying beneath him, drawing him deep into herself. She thought she had finally found the man of her dreams. What she didn't know was that George had this history of leaving after five days. Laura was history-in-the-making.

"Don't ever leave me," she begged.

George was already gone. To some deep corner of his mind, where he hid among shadows and dreams. He was also thinking about the symposium a friend had convinced him he needed, and about the vision of his love life of the future. Unlike Martha, he had no difficulty with visions. He was an actor, always making up movies in his mind.

"Slower, slower, baby."

Faster, faster, his mind raced around the world for a suitable location. Hawaii, Bali, Fiji, the Greek Islands. He let the camera roll and, as always, the right scene came into focus. By the sea somewhere, a huge villa, a beach below. Two lovers, he and his ideal mate, climbing up a path, the sun setting on their backs, sinking into the blue waters. Dolphins dancing, an angel on an olive tree, doves, the sound of a harp, a flute. The two lovers embraced in golden light.

The next morning Philip was gone. Martha, excited for the first time in months, sat down to type up her vision. She was still confused, however. Part of her wanted to paint it, not write it. And she wondered if by not painting it, she would put more pressure on the universe to make it real for her. Maybe God was the master painter and He took suggestions from the audience. And she was still frustrated by the very concept of visions, where they came from, what they meant and who had the right to have them. She wondered if maybe she was a visionary after all, and had been one all her life. She wondered if everyone was a visionary who had been taught not to believe.

She typed up her vision.

George slipped out of Laura's embrace at dawn. He got dressed, tiptoed out of her Eastside condominium and took a cab down to Battery Park, where he watched the sun rise over Brooklyn.

He scribbled his vision of the future on a note pad, feeling incredibly empty inside. Whenever he left a relationship, he felt this lonely, longing tug at his heart, as though he were abandoning a part of himself each time. If so, he had abandoned so many parts of himself he wondered if there was anything left worth preserving.

He continued his scribbling.

George had no problems with visions. He knew he wasn't a visionary, never even considered the possibility. On the other hand, he had this golden touch. His dreams always came true. With uncanny regularity. Only problem was what looked good to his imagination seemed destined for defeat in his life.

He had no doubt that he could make this movie he imagined. He just wasn't sure he wanted the part.

When she completed her vision, Martha was feeling high and optimistic. Who knows, she thought. It was Friday afternoon, and the symposium began that evening. She had one thing to do first.

She had to pick up her dog at the vet's, then drop her off with a friend for the weekend. Lulu was a fifteen-year-old border collie who had been Martha's faithful companion all her life. She had brought her to Dr. Epstein two days ago for a stomach virus.

When she arrived at the doctor's office, she could tell immediately that something was wrong. For one thing, Dr. Epstein did not come out to greet her as he always did. They had dated several years back, and although romance was not their purpose, a warm friendship had resulted.

Also, she could not feel Lulu's presence anywhere in the office, and that was strange.

Finally, Dr. Epstein emerged to tell her the bad news. Lulu was dying. Stomach cancer. Nothing to be done.

Martha was stunned, all her optimism suddenly despair. As the good doctor put the dog to sleep, she cried on his shoulder. Then she went home and cried in her pillow. Then she looked at her vision and decided to add the part about Lulu coming back from the dead. What the hell, she thought.

As she headed for the symposium, she felt schizophrenic. One moment she was in utter hopelessness, feeling like everything was being taken away from her, that she'd never get her life straightened out. The next moment she'd be full of excitement and expectation, as though something new and wonderful were about to enter her life.

Maybe she had paid her dues by releasing Philip and sacrificing Lulu. Maybe all this loss was somehow necessary in preparation for some unknown gain. Surely, the gods owed her something, that is if the gods could ever be in debt to humans.

George arrived at the relationships symposium still scribbling his vision on a napkin. He was coming from an audition and his mind was more on Thomas Jefferson in "1776" than the future of his love life. Hardly *Hamlet*, but big time Broadway for sure.

He considered leaving the seminar before it started, but that seemed like his problem with women in general. Leaving at the beginning. So he headed for the registration table, resigned if not enthusiastic. He didn't see the girl in the red dress when he brushed against her. And when he looked up, she was turning towards him, it seemed, in slow motion. He thought he recognized her way of turning. Something. It took his breath away.

"Déjà vu?" he laughed as their eyes locked.

Martha blushed and then denied it to herself. She was thinking, what an arrogant bastard! And she walked off in a huff.

They didn't know it, but they were already veering in the same direction. They each had their own version, but the vision itself foretold the same dream come true, and was already in the process of drawing them together.

WAY #1: SEEING WITH YOUR EYES CLOSED

Your vision is your ticket to the future. Your guiding light. Hold this vision to your heart and it will steer you through thick and thin, move you in the right direction and deliver you to a new reality. Start with a happy ending.

Often we tend to enter a new relationship without any idea of where we want it to go. We know what we don't want, but have we ever stopped to define what we do want? What you focus on in your mind expands in your experience. Alfred Hitchcock planned every detail of his films before he started shooting. He saw the finished product, then started at the beginning and knew where he was headed.

There is a difference between vision and fantasy. Fantasy exists solely in the mind. Its very nature is unreality. Its purpose is to provide escape from what is perceived as a cold, cruel world, a safety valve when the going gets rough. Fantasies are based on wishes, hopes, fairy tales— they are filled with knights on white horses and damsels in distress. They are neither here nor now. How could they be? If they were, they wouldn't be fantasies. Reality can often be fantastic, but fantasy can never be real.

On the other hand, dreams can come true. You can have it all—have that ideal loving relationship that lasts forever. You can evolve a vision of your life and step into that vision, become a visionary and manifest a reality that reflects your vision.

Start your relationship with a vision of its end—its ultimate reality, its happy results. Once you do that, you can take the necessary steps to achieve those ends. Without vision you are walking in the dark, blind in love, groping for solutions you have no faith in.

We all need a dream to hitch our lucky stars to.

AFFIRMATIONS

1. *I am a visionary at heart.*
2. *My faith in the future is greater than my regrets about the past.*
3. *I have a vision God guides me towards.*
4. *My vision is now clear.*
5. *I can see my future.*
6. *I now release all fantasies and desires to escape.*
7. *I forgive myself for hiding in fantasy in order to avoid reality.*
8. *My reality is fantastic.*
9. *Miracles abound in my life.*
10. *My love life gets better every day.*
11. *I am a romantic realist; my reality is romantic.*
12. *I love the reality of love.*
13. *I attract the perfect partner to share my vision with.*
14. *I have more than enough time to realize my vision.*
15. *My vision keeps me youthful.*
16. *I never compromise my vision.*
17. *I accept the process my vision guides me through.*
18. *I am committed to making my dream come true.*
19. *My vision is exciting to dwell on.*
20. *My vision heals me and my partner.*

—2—

Leave Your Leaving Pattern Behind

It was 1966, before EST, Lifespring, LRT, Rolfing, Rebirthing, Reflexology and a host of other self-improvement seminars and techniques would sweep the country. The Beatles were just meeting Maharishi. LSD was reaching out to TM. The New Age, as it would come to be called, was still in the womb. We were looking to the East, yes, but more towards Vietnam than India. And on the streets, riots, rebellion and rock 'n roll defined the decade.

I called my little symposium Relationships 2000. My purpose was to assist individuals who were ready to be pioneers in the arena of human relationships. It was necessary, I felt, to start with one's personal life and then to extend outwards. Everyone was trying to change the world those days, but they hadn't bothered to change themselves first. The result was a massive projection of unresolved personal issues onto political authorities. Instead of taking real responsibility for change, people were acting out years of suppressed rage which they suddenly gave themselves permission to express. The result was chaos more than cleansing, confusion more than clarity.

We were entering the last third of the twentieth century. Technology was advancing in quantum leaps. Yet our knowledge of human relationships was still bogged down in the Middle Ages. It was time to stretch into new dimensions of relationships just as passionately as we were exploring outer space.

8

It was early June. George and Martha were two of fifty-two partici-pants in my weekend symposium. The format was largely experiential. The group would break up into sub-groups, pairs, teams of six and ten, to study their own belief systems as well as new ideas about relation-ships. I also offered some data. On Friday night I asked the group: "How many of you would like to change the world?" Almost everyone raised their hands. Then I flipped my flip chart and a bold statement was printed in red ink: "Anything unresolved in your personal life will attempt to obstruct your desire to change the world!" You had to start with your-self, I told them, with your mental health, with your attitudes toward your mother, father, siblings—the first people you formed relationships with. You may be carrying a backlog of pain from the past into your dream of the future. To get clear on the future you had to clear out the past first. There were several hisses from the participants. I joked that I was glad we had several snakes in the audience since this was a sympo-sium on evolution. Maybe we could climb out of the age of reptile rela-tionships. There was some laughter.

Then I asked each person in the group to pair up with a buddy. This would be someone with whom they would practice a relationship of the future. Whether it turned out to be a friendship, a business association or an intimate relationship, their context for relating would be 2000 A.D.

By sheer coincidence or divine providence, George and Martha chose each other. I noticed the two of them doing the initial exercise, sharing (1) their first impressions of each other, and (2) their visions for their lives in the twenty-first century. They seemed an attractive team: he tall, blonde, and athletic; she also tall and blonde, with a dancer's body. They were both outgoing, alive, and energetically equal. I remember thinking, "You never know."

At the first break, Martha came up to me and demanded a new buddy. She was clearly activated.

"But why?" I asked.

"I don't like him. He's conceited, arrogant and . . . too damn seductive!"

"It sounds like you're afraid you like him."

"I can't stand him!" she shouted, as other particpants turned to look. "Besides, he's not serious about being here. He's got his vision scribbled on napkins and his mind's preoccupied with this dumb part he just au-ditioned for. I want someone who'll be there for me."

"Give him a chance."

"It's a mistake to put me with him. It will ruin my whole weekend."

I reminded Martha that I hadn't put them together. They had. And I repeated what I had told the whole group, that there were no accidents and that by the end of the weekend they would understand the unconscious reasons that drew them to their buddies. Martha was not impressed.

"Bullshit!" she said, and stormed off.

After the break, when the group was settled, I briefed them on what they could expect to experience during the symposium—the desire to leave, skepticism, boredom, projections, strong feeling, and so forth. Then I discussed communication, the art of telling the truth fast and listening without defense, saying what you mean and meaning what you say, and explained how we would handle sharing. Instantly, George's hand went up like a jack-in-the-box. I called on him and he stood up.

"I want to leave."

"Good," I replied. "You're already processing your leaving pattern."

"No, I mean it," he persisted. "You said to tell the truth fast so I'm doing it. I don't want to be here. I think this is a con act. I'm pissed off that I signed up in the first place. And . . ." his voice trailed off.

"And what, George?"

"And . . ."

"George. The whole truth and nothing but the truth, so help you God."

"And I want a new buddy."

"So do I!" Martha had jumped up even though I had instructed the group not to cross-share. Now, everyone was buzzing, amused and aroused by this interaction, and obviously curious to see how I would handle the situation.

"This hardly sounds like a relationship of the future."

"It isn't," cried Martha. "This guy's ancient history for me."

"Thank you for sharing, Martha," I said. "But it's George's turn now. I'll get to you later." Martha sat down in a huff, and everyone giggled.

"George," I continued, "what's the main thing you want to get from this workshop?"

"A new buddy?" he joked, and the group laughed.

"Seriously."

"I guess I want to learn how to stay in a relationship, not to run away from women who love me."

"Thank you."

"The truth is I have a wicked leaving pattern. I mean, when you were talking about leaving patterns, I was sure you were talking to me and no one else in the room."

George's honesty was impulsive and, yes, seductive. "I mean, I really have a furious leaving pattern."

"You mean you always leave furious?" I half-joked.

"Well, yes, that too."

"What's the longest relationship you've ever had?"

"Well, let's see, one, two . . . I'd say six days." The group was laughing wildly, and George and I were eating it up.

"Six days?"

"Five nights, to be precise. In fact, I always leave on the sixth morning."

I took a breath and felt my compassion for George. I could feel his pain for all the times he ran away from women he loved, the pain he felt he caused them, the pain he caused himself. And from my compassion, as I had learned to trust, my intuition spoke through me. Knowing nothing, I asked point-blank, "When did your dad leave your mom, George?"

"Well, that's an interesting question. Actually, I didn't have a dad."

"Come on, George, we all had dads. You weren't an immaculate conception, were you?"

"No." George's whole composure shifted, and in the shift a powerful feeling was bubbling to the surface. "I never knew my dad because he left six days after he met my mom. He was in the Navy. He married my mom on leave in Honolulu. Then he went off and got killed at Pearl Harbor."

A hush filled the room. George was crying, crying for a father he had never seen.

"My mom always cries when she remembers—six days of heaven, she calls it."

"George, did it ever occur to you that your father's tragic death is the source of your furious leaving pattern, and that beneath the fury is the pain?"

"But I never knew him."

"Yet you're crying. Your body knew him."

"I guess."

"George, I think you should stick it out with Martha."

"I guess."

"Is that okay, Martha?" She didn't stand up. Her energy had changed from seeing George so vulnerable.

"Yes. I'm sorry."

After the symposium, George and Martha became private clients of mine. When they were on the road, they called me frequently or wrote, and so I was able to keep informed on the incredible changes they were to experience. Little did I know it at the time, but this unlikely couple would become the most successful graduates of Relationships 2000.

Way #2: Leave Your Leaving Pattern Behind

Leave your leaving pattern behind. This whole book is about leaving your leaving pattern, but if you're not willing to leave it in the first place, you will leave this book incomplete, your addiction to running away still greater than your desire to stay in love.

It's safe to stay. It really is. We all have furious leaving patterns, or patterns of being abandoned, two sides of the same coin. Take heart! What is a pattern but unconscious, repetitive behavior? Becoming conscious of an unconscious, automatic response threatens nothing but your ego, your attraction to fear and negative thought forms. In truth there is nothing to fear from knowing yourself. Awareness will release you. Consciousness will set you free.

Things that contribute to a leaving pattern, things that you want to become aware of, things we will cover in the course of this book include: family patterns, birth scripts, unconscious death urge, intimacy threshold, fear of loss, need to be in control, power trips, revenge, guilt, attack thoughts, denial, and low self-esteem.

Pretty heavy stuff.

But becoming enlightened about your problems is, first of all, lightening up. Taking the heavy stuff lightly, the weight you bear with a sense of the absurd, is the first step towards resolution of the past, solutions to present problems and success in the future.

So, lighten up, reader. Don't take your life too personally. After all, you can run away from your unconscious self all you want. It will always follow you.

You might as well learn to live with yourself, laugh at your woes (most of our soap operas are situation comedies in disguise), and clear the way.

In the end the only one you can't leave is yourself. Why would you even want to try?

AFFIRMATIONS

1. *My desire to surrender is greater than my fear of loss.*
2. *It's safe to stay.*
3. *I only leave when it no longer serves my higher purpose to stay.*
4. *I can stay longer than I think.*
5. *I can survive staying.*
6. *The more I play, the more I stay.*
7. *The more I stay, the more I play.*
8. *The more I laugh, the longer love lasts.*
9. *I can see the light at the end of any tunnel.*
10. *Since light is my goal, I might as well lighten up now.*
11. *I no longer postpone joy and aliveness.*
12. *My joy and aliveness are a pleasure to others.*
13. *I can stay as long as I want.*
14. *I can surpass my family pattern of staying and leaving.*
15. *I no longer leave compulsively or angrily.*
16. *I no longer create conflict to justify leaving.*
17. *It's safe when things get good.*
18. *I can handle lots of love.*
19. *I choose to stay in love.*
20. *I never leave the self I choose to face.*

—3—

There's Always a Way Out

It was the morning of the sixth day. George was preparing to leave.

He had been with Martha ever since the symposium. Couldn't keep his hands off her. He had never felt anything like this before. Nor had she.

Although it was less than a week, they had gone through so much together it seemed like lifetimes. Maybe it was. They were already talking moving in, marriage, children, the whole works. Major commitment stuff.

George felt his style cramped. He thought of himself as a free spirit, a man in the moment, ready, willing and able to seize the next opportunity life offered. Settling down seemed to oppose his very nature. If a drifter stopped drifting, his waters grew stagnant. And stagnancy terrified him.

On the other hand, he was drawn to Martha like a tide to the shore. Anything but stagnant. He could no more walk away from her than a wave could stop breaking. There was some inexorable force at work here and they both knew it was bigger than both of them.

Still, his mind kept getting in the way, telling him it was a trap, he needed breathing room, a chance to think it over.

"You're married to your freedom," Martha said.

"I'm not ready to annul it."

"You think freedom is leaving."

"Birds fly."

"They also build nests."

George was packing a suitcase. In fact, he was leaving for the Williamstown Playhouse where he had a good summer stock job. This had all been arranged months before, had nothing to do with Martha. It was just a coincidence that this was the sixth morning.

"Coincidence, my ass," said Martha.

"You think I planned leaving you before I met you?"

"I wouldn't put it past you."

He turned towards her. She was naked except for her pink panties, and her long, languorous body glistened with a vibrant sensuality. They embraced.

"I love you, Martha."

"Let me come with you."

"I won't have time for you."

"I won't mind."

"I will. I need to focus on my work."

"So, focus."

She drew him to the bed, where they spent the next hour in silent bliss. Now they lay on their backs, wondering where to go from here. They sighed simultaneously, no solution emerging. George sat up and began to get dressed.

"Don't leave."

"I'll be back in six weeks."

"Are you sure I shouldn't come?"

"No, I'm not sure. The only thing I'm sure about is that I'm not leaving."

"No?"

"No. I'm going, but I'm not leaving."

"I see."

She believed him. Somewhere inside herself she was certain he would return, certain that she needed to give him this space alone, a space to choose freely, to blow with the wind and let the wind blow him back to her. She was certain but, on the other hand, she thought it was all foolish, that freedom had nothing to do with coming and going, that it was really an internal state. She remembered reading about people in prison who, in the solitude of their cells, had discovered a deeper freedom than most so-called free people. When you're free in your mind, you're free in your life, she thought. But she kept her mouth shut, knowing this was a necessary step in George's choice to be with her. If he didn't feel that choice, nothing would work.

George was thinking about the seminar, wondering how he and Martha came to choose each other as buddies.

"I wonder why we chose each other."

"It's a mystery to me."

"Maybe it's love that's the mystery."

"Yeah, maybe we love the mystery, not each other."

"Could be."

"That's it, we're all closet detectives at heart."

"Profound."

They stopped in silence again, transfixed by each other's gaze. It was one of those eternal pauses they were learning to honor.

George was ready to go. But he knew he wasn't leaving.

WAY #3: THERE'S ALWAYS A WAY OUT

There's always a way out. You're always free to leave. You're free to come and go as you please. Nobody can take that away from you. In the end, there is no escape from freedom.

Freedom, however, is not running off all the time. That's not free, that's compulsive leaving, going on automatic, acting like a robot. You can't be free if you're totally predictable. Flying off every six days, nine months, or three years is a habit, not freedom.

True freedom is knowledge, consciousness of yourself. The more aware you become of your unconscious self—the part of the iceberg that's beneath the surface—the more power you have to choose freely, to break old habits, to change. Sometimes, a convict in a prison cell can find the freedom a so-called free man can't. The reason is he has looked within, or to God, and has come to understand that liberty and freedom are two different things.

Your thoughts are creative and you are the thinker. Freedom is releasing counter-productive negative thoughts from your mind so you don't have to act them out over and over again. You are free to think whatever you want, to select the highest quality thoughts you can.

Freedom and commitment are not polar opposites as they sometimes seem. They are twins—the more you freely choose to follow your own heart, the more your heart guides you to appropriate choices. All appropriate choices are commitments you have freely made.

And yes, you are free to leave any time you want. There's always a way out, and often just knowing the door is open makes it easier to stay. The choice is yours, every moment of your life. You're free as a bird. To fly or to build a nest.

AFFIRMATIONS

1. *Thank God I'm free.*

2. *I'm free to do as I please.*

3. *I'm free of compulsive habits.*

4. *I need nobody's permission to do as I please.*

5. *Being in love supports my freedom.*

6. *Love sets me free.*

7. *Love is freedom.*

8. *There's always a way out.*

9. *I'm never bound by love.*

10. *Love is unlimited, it gives me more space.*

11. *My first commitment is to myself.*

12. *My freedom is safe for me and everyone else.*

13. *My freedom is a pleasure for me and those I love.*

14. *Since I know I can always leave, I only stay freely.*

15. *The more I choose to stay, the more space I have to stay in.*

16. *I am committed to my own freedom.*

17. *The more I choose freely, the more free I feel.*

18. *The more I choose out of limited thinking, the freer I become.*

19. *I no longer have to separate to feel free.*

20. *Two people can be free together.*

—4—

Slowly Is Holy
(Fear Forward)

Martha was an artist. She worked as an illustrator for McGraw-Hill and lived in Westbeth in the West Village. Her loft overlooked the Hudson River, and even though she had no great fondness for New Jersey, the sunsets were terrific. For Martha, there was no place like home.

She stood by her easel and examined her latest painting-in-progress. It was her vision for her life in the year 2000. She had completed a section of the foreground, where two dolphins were leaping out of the sea. Now she was working on the olive tree with the cherub and the two doves in midair.

As she painted her ideal, she was distracted by reality. George had returned from Williamstown, and their relationship resumed with all the passion and magic of the first five days. Thinking of George, she started to shake. Was it excitement or fear, she didn't know. She put down her brush and walked out on the balcony. She thought about last night.

Maybe she had been wrong to insist that George move in with her. She didn't want to be the "heavy" in this relationship. Her pattern had been quick starts, abrupt endings. She wanted this one to be different. But George was so wishy-washy. He had had his six weeks in Williamstown. He said he wanted to be with her. Moving in made sense.

She had no idea why she was suddenly sobbing uncontrollably.

George hadn't cried in ages, until now. He plopped down on his bed and buried his head in his pillow so he wouldn't have to hear the sound of his sadness.

He lived in the Village also, on Thompson Street in an old Italian neighborhood. He had a fifth floor walk-up, a railroad flat and, at $75 per month, considered it the real estate coup of the century. He loved his local inconspicuous bistro, his funky laundromat, his little grocery store, his ethnic neighbors. Even though he had landed a regular part on "As the World Turns," as well as a lead role in "1776," and could easily afford a more luxurious environment, George was perfectly content with his simple home. He had no desire in the world to move. Least of all in with Martha.

Then why was he crying? He wondered if he had blown the whole thing last night. After all, he did want Martha, more than he had ever wanted anyone. He didn't want to be the "heavy" in this relationship. He didn't want to be wishy-washy. He just wanted to move slowly. How could he have this relationship if she had her foot on the accelerator and he had his on the brake?

When George called, I had not spoken to him since the day before he left for Williamstown, when he had called to ask my opinion on his leaving Martha for six weeks.

"She wants me to move in," he exploded on the phone even before I recognized his voice.

"Excuse me?"

"It's George. Martha demands that I move in yesterday. For Christ's sake, I just got back to town. What's going on, doc?"

"How was Williamstown?"

"Super. Except for Martha. I mean, except for missing her and not being able to get her out of my mind."

"You still want her?"

"Oh yeah. But we only had five days, you know."

"Afraid to surpass your dad?"

"No."

"Afraid to surpass yourself?"

"Getting warm."

"What is it then?"

"Just plain afraid. Afraid of love, afraid of women, afraid period."

"Fear forward, George."

"You mean, you think I should move in?"

"Not necessarily. I never tell people what they should do. My suggestion is that you handle your fear and Martha handle her urgency. Think of it this way. Martha represents your mother wanting your dad to stay. She's pregnant with you and doesn't want him to go off and get killed in the war. The anxiety you're feeling is in your cellular roots."

"My what?"

"Why don't you make an appointment with me to deal with your prenatal script?"

"My what?"

"I'll explain when I see you. How's Friday at noon?"

"Sounds good. My place or yours?"

"Mine, George. This is a session, not a date."

"One more thing, doc. Do you think Martha and I have a chance?"

"Sure you have a chance. Whether you take it or not is completely up to the two of you."

Later that day Martha rang me up with her version of the story, which was not that different from George's. A good sign, I thought. At least they're not distorting reality.

"Slow down," I urged her.

"Why? I love him. He loves me. Why put off the inevitable?"

"Because your urgency is pushing him away."

"You think I'm wrong for wanting him so much?"

"No. You're not wrong. You're just frantic. And whenever I'm frantic, it's well worth my while to slow down and take a good look at what's really going on."

"I can't imagine you frantic."

"I have my moments."

"Well, what do you think is really going on?"

"I think you're afraid of losing George and want to tie the knot before he escapes."

"Men always leave me," she sighed with resignation.

"That's just a thought, Martha."

"But it's true."

"Of course it's true."

"Are you telling me that my dad rejected me because I thought so, and Philip, and now George?"

"Wait a minute. George has not rejected you, and, as for the others, yes."

"You're saying I'm not a victim."

"For sure."

"And that if I change my attitude, I'll get different results."

"You bet."

"I feel like you're giving me this magic wand and I don't even believe in magic."

"Of course you do."

"I used to."

"Relax, Martha. Take your time. Slowly is holy."

"I never knew slow, not since my birth. Labor took twenty-four hours. I was breech. I think I've been trying to make up for lost time ever since."

"Or avoid the pain."

"What do you mean?"

"I think it would be good if I saw you privately. You're sitting on a breath release."

"A what?"

"How's Friday at four?"

"Okay."

"Great. See you then."

"Just talk to George about moving in, will you? He's so scared."

WAY #4: SLOWLY IS HOLY (FEAR FORWARD)

Slowly is holy. Take your time. The urgency to possess a person you love actually drives him (her) away and is a function of your own subconscious fear of abandonment.

Take it one day at a time, if that fast.

I've had middle-aged clients who've confessed to me that they rushed into relationships so fast that before they knew it they were married with kids and obligations they never wanted.

Love is one thing. A relationship is something else. The ideal is to let one grow out of the other, organically, at its own natural pace and rhythm.

Don't form entanglements in the physical universe that exceed your honest desires. In other words, don't share a home, money, bills, children, etc., before you are comfortable handling that much energy and responsibility in a relationship.

An entanglement is when the demonstration part of the relationship goes beyond the feeling part. That's when you begin to feel trapped, obligated, restricted. That's when you feel like you've lost your freedom. Nobody's taken it away but you.

Once entangled, you're still free to leave, but it's much more complicated when you've strapped yourself down with a lot of agreements you never should have made in the first place.

Slowly is holy.

On the other hand, if you have a basic fear of jumping in, fear forward. If you tend to hold yourself back, let yourself go. Take risks. Risks are chances, and chances are opportunities. If you never take a leap, you never find out how high you can fly, let alone where you might land.

If you're always in a rush, cool it. Take your foot off the accelerator. If you're always cautious, take your foot off the brake.

One thing is certain: never drive with one foot on the accelerator and the other on the brake. You'll just waste gas and spin your wheels.

AFFIRMATIONS

1. *The more I take my time, the more time I have to take.*

2. *Time is on my side.*

3. *I have more than enough time to accomplish all my heart's desires.*

4. *Since I've already made it, I can relax and enjoy it.*

5. *I can survive going slow.*

6. *I am no longer threatened by slowing down.*

7. *The more I slow down, the faster things come to me.*

8. *Since I deserve what I want, I no longer have to chase it.*

9. *I have it all coming to me.*

10. *I am a magnet; the more I slow down, the more I attract good things.*

11. *Since nobody wants to leave me, I no longer have to hold on to anyone.*

12. *People stay with me as long as I want.*

13. *It's safe to take risks.*

14. *I take advantage of every opportunity.*

15. *I can survive without holding myself back.*

16. *Fear is an invitation to move forward faster.*

17. *I'm safe even when I'm frightened.*

18. *I can succeed at things that frighten me.*

19. *When I step through my fears, I stretch into greater safety.*

20. *It's safe to jump in quickly.*

—5—

Unearth Your Birth

George's mother, Elizabeth Brewer, was eighteen when she got pregnant. Oliver Rome was a sailor on leave in Honolulu, where young Elizabeth was studying Japanese brush stroke at the university. She met Oliver one night at a local bar, fell for his Gary Cooper good looks and his Cary Grant bravura, and went to bed with him after too many Black Russians. As he made love to her, he told her she looked like Marlene Dietrich. No wonder their son turned out to be an actor.

Their relationship was like a rocket. It blasted off, then was gone. They made noisy love for five straight days, and on the fifth day the condom broke. The next day he was gone. One hour before he took off, they were married by a local kahuna.

Oliver Rome was killed in action at Pearl Harbor one week later, December 7, 1941.

As George lay on his back, breathing under my guidance, he could feel himself in his mother's womb. For most unborn babies, the prenatal nine months is a time of tremendous joy and excitement, love and growth. Not so for George. It was all mourning for him. Elizabeth could not stop weeping. Oliver, the love of her life, was dead, and she had never gotten to know him. The loss tore her to pieces and George could feel the painful fragments passing from her to him.

Elizabeth was hardly ready for motherhood. When she was three months pregnant, she sailed home to her parents in Los Angeles, and they arranged an abortion. It was when she was about to board the train to Tijuana that she decided she could not go through with it. Not because she wanted a baby, but because she feared the abortion.

George could feel the abortion thought shudder through his body as he breathed. He couldn't stop crying. He was in mourning for his life. His session was so poignant I felt tears come to my eyes several times.

George was late. Three weeks late. He procrastinated because he didn't want to come out. Would you? His mother was petite and frightened, and he was big and didn't want to hurt her. Moreover, he didn't want to be a burden, and what else could he be? He remembered thinking, even in the womb, that he had come too soon, that it would be better if he died and came back at a later date. He wasn't sure if these were his thoughts or his mother's, or whether it made a difference.

George could feel the walls of the uterus closing in on him. No exit terror. "I've got to get out of here," he thought, at the same moment wishing he weren't there at all, or anywhere for that matter. He could hear a doctor and a nurse discussing what to do next. When they decided to induce him, he dug his fingers into his mother's flesh and he could hear her scream. Then, when they actually induced him, all hell broke loose. It was an avalanche of sensation, tidal waves and earthquakes, tornadoes and landslides. George could feel himself being shoved out against his will.

He didn't want to leave, but he had to get out. So, finally, when he seemed to have no choice, he let go and rode the big wave out.

Then it all stopped. He was stuck in the middle. He couldn't turn back and there was no light at the end. He twisted and turned. He seemed to sense that it was a false tranquility, that the storm would return.

If only they would just leave him alone. But that was the last thing on their minds. The obstetrician thought this baby was in trouble, that he might not make it at all, and that he definitely needed some mechanical help. George was growing angrier and angrier.

In desperation he wrapped the cord around his neck. At this point in the session I could see a thin red line appear around his throat, as if a hidden scar were made visible by his breath. George then stopped breathing altogether. His face lost all color, then turned blue and purple. Suddenly, he reached for his head and screamed:

"My head! My head!"

I could see the forceps marks on his temples. He began coughing uncontrollably. I encouraged him to relax and connect with his breath again, and then he took off. His breathing stopped being mechanical, the struggle disappeared, and he was soaring on a spontaneous breath, rising and falling rapidly, sending waves of energy through his body, building to a huge crescendo, releasing the tension in his throat and then, at last, subsiding into more gentle waves of warm tingling light. He started to laugh.

"Wow!" he said.

"Wow," I confirmed.

After the session, George wanted to know what it all meant. He felt terrific, excited, alive, all his senses fresh with new smells, tastes, colors, sounds, and feelings. He kept touching his face like a newborn. He thought he felt like a peach and smelled like a watermelon, his mother's favorite fruit. But what did it all mean?

I was always reluctant to interpret my clients' birth experiences. I preferred them to make their own associations, draw their own conclusions. That way they integrated more. What they discovered was their own. What I saw was my projection. I tried to keep the two separate.

"What do you think?" I asked.

"Well, I felt it all—the mourning, the abortion, the induction, the cord, the forceps. The funny thing is I feel it all all the time. Especially when a woman wants me. I mean, Martha is inducing me and I'm all tied up in knots like at my birth. Jesus! It's all the same. I'm late. I procrastinate, I've got to get out or I'll die. And the last thing I want is to hurt her."

"You survived your birth, George. You can survive a loving relationship."

"I feel like I let go of a shitload of fear, I'll tell you that."

"You did."

"Will it come back?"

"Only if you revert to the old thoughts."

"Thought is creative, eh doc?"

"You bet your life it is."

"I better keep an eye on my mind."

"You do that, and love will never be blind."

"But doc, how do I know it's true, any of it? Maybe I made it all up."

"Ask your mother."

George telephoned his mother that night, and she corroborated the entire story of his birth.

Way #5: Unearth Your Birth

The first place you left was your mother's womb, so if you want to leave your leaving pattern behind, it stands to reason that you should make peace with your birth. The reason we bury our primal experience is that it is so powerful we don't want to experience it again. But when you create the safety to go through your birth again, such as in rebirthing, you free yourself from a whole lot of myths you've been imposing on life.

These birth memories are lodged in both your subconscious mind and your cellular memory bank. They are accessible, as any unconscious programming is retrievable, given the right coaching and environment. And since your thoughts are creative, locating and changing the first set of beliefs you chose about life can alter your entire context for experiencing the world and the relationships you have in it.

It might be that the panic we feel around separation is always, on some level, the subconscious fear of reliving the moment when the umbilical cord, our apparent source of life in the womb, was abruptly severed. For most of us the cutting of the cord was so sudden it made our first breath excruciatingly difficult. This is why we see babies gagging and coughing, turning blue and spitting up amniotic fluid as they struggle for the breath of life. No wonder birth and death are so intimate in our imagination. If the cord were not cut so hastily, the baby would have the umbilical safety system available while it took its time to discover breathing with its lungs. This usually does not take more than five minutes.

In any case, birth is our first major change in life, and since it colors all our major transitions with a life-or-death shadow, it is extremely practical to rid ourselves of these buried memories once and for all.

No, you cannot change your birth. And no, it is not opening a can of worms to retrieve this experience. The truth is somewhere in the middle. You can change and improve your life and relationships by locating and releasing your primal pain and the first choices you made about life and people, choices which may no longer serve your desired results.

For further information read Birth and Relationships, *and call the Rebirthing Hotline at 1-800-INTL-LRT, or 203-354-8509.*

AFFIRMATIONS

1. *I no longer have to re-create my birth script in my relationships.*

2. *I forgive my obstetrician for separating me from my mother.*

3. *It's safe to be separate from my mother.*

4. *I can relax in the midst of change.*

5. *The unknown is safe.*

6. *I no longer have to leave to continue growing.*

7. *The more I breathe, the less suffocated I feel.*

8. *I no longer project my mother on my partner.*

9. *I survived my birth; I can survive a long, loving relationship.*

10. *My aliveness is a pleasure for me and everyone else.*

11. *I have a purpose in being here.*

12. *I am always where I should be at the right time.*

13. *I am free of the panic of birth.*

14. *It's easy for me to let go.*

15. *I am wanted.*

16. *I am God's gift to the world.*

17. *My presence adds happiness to the lives of those I love.*

18. *Thank God I've made it.*

19. *I no longer have to struggle to make it.*

20. *My relationship is a womb which grows with me.*

—6—

Break the Law

Martha's session was an altogether different matter. She arrived a half hour late, dressed to kill in a red halter top and tight shorts, with makeup so excessive that it diminished her natural beauty. As soon as she started breathing, she thought she was doing it wrong and said so. When I assured her she was going great guns, an ancient sadness poured out of her.

Martha was the firstborn of three girls. Her dad, Alex Kaplan, a prominent Los Angeles entertainment attorney, wanted a boy, was certain he'd have a boy (he always got what he wanted) and bet his certainty to the tune of fifty grand. Martha's mother, Sarah, was furious with her husband for gambling on the gender of their child. In fact, she considered leaving him altogether during the pregnancy.

Martha somehow felt all this turmoil in the womb. She could hear them screaming at each other and would reach her hands to her ears in the fluid that surrounded her. Once her mother packed her bags to leave but fell down a staircase almost causing a miscarriage. Martha clung for dear life, knowing she was unwanted as a girl and there was nothing she would ever be able to do about it. Why she clung to life she could not imagine.

No wonder she was a breech birth. She twisted herself around, hoping to hide her sex from the world. She was supposed to be born at home. Her parents wanted a natural childbirth, but because of the near miscarriage and the complications at the last minute, she was rushed off to a hospital. Her father demanded to be in the delivery room, but when he was refused entry he stormed off to the closest bar to down bourbon and sodas and dream about his son being the next Lou Gehrig. He was, quite honestly, more concerned about winning his bet than about the health of his wife and child.

Martha was delivered by two female obstetricians, a fact that had made her trust women more than men her entire life. As she breathed in my presence, she cried, "Men are never there for me," and then, "I'm wrong for being a woman," and finally, "I cost men a fortune." Some way to start a life!

She cried incessantly throughout her session. She wanted me to hold her, hug her, and then even make love to her, she was so desperate to feel wanted as a woman. I did all I could do, short of touching her, to support her self-esteem. To give her that physical cuddling might have comforted her in the short run, but in the end I knew it would have ripped her off.

When it was over, she said, "That was amazing."

"You are amazing."

"I feel like I know who I am for the first time."

"Don't try to make sense of it too soon."

"Suddenly my whole life makes sense. I felt so unwanted as a woman, so wrong, so ugly—I think I created all that rejection just so I could be right about being wrong."

"Well, all roads led you to George."

"Oh God, don't let him reject me."

"I think you should consider forgiving your father."

"The bastard!"

"You love the bastard. Even in the womb you wanted to please him. You came out backwards because you were ashamed of yourself as a female."

"I cost him a small fortune."

"Your life is priceless, though."

"I've tried to be a boy my whole life. I was a jock, an A student, I went to law school, then quit after I was first in my class. I even have fantasies about having a penis."

"It's called your Primal Law, Martha. Your most negative thought about yourself. In your mind, you've been wrong for being a woman. That one thought has sucked your self-esteem out of you, pushed men away. Your only solution was to overcompensate, beat men at their own game. Only that didn't work either."

"Jesus, I've been so blind."

"You've got to break that law, Martha. Start thinking you're right as a woman; build a new structure from that foundation."

"It's like starting all over again, isn't it?"

"You've got so much to start with, Martha. You're beautiful, intelligent, alive. God don't make mistakes, you know. Your dad, maybe. God, never."

Martha laughed.

"My dad just had a dumb hunch, huh?"

"Yeah. Maybe his Primal Law is, 'I'm dumb as a man.'"

WAY #6: BREAK THE LAW

Your Primal Law is the emergency brake you won't let go of. How can you accelerate when you're stuck in your most negative thought about yourself? When you're stalled in low self-esteem, how can anyone else think you're the greatest? How can anyone love you fully when you're going around thinking, I'm wrong or I'm evil or I'm guilty or I'm unwanted or I don't belong or I'm unlovable or I'm unworthy.

Such laws repel many a potential partner. You attract a lover who loves you and the love brings up anything unlike itself for healing, namely your self-hate glued to your Primal Law. The choice is clear. Let it go or let him or her go—you can't have both as lovers.

Break the law!

It's the biggest lie you're holding about yourself, an erroneous conclusion you made about yourself at birth, learned by heart, and repeated unconsciously time after time. Wake up! Take a good look at yourself. There's nothing wrong with you that a healthy dose of self-love won't fix.

God don't make junk!

Affirmations

1. I love myself unconditionally.
2. I have so much going for me.
3. Thank God I'm me.
4. I am now the person I always wanted to be like.
5. I'm "Number One."
6. There's no one else on earth like me.
7. I'm one-of-a-kind.
8. I am a unique part of God's plan.
9. I am the right sex.
10. I am wanted for who I am.
11. I am irresistible.
12. I am more than good enough for myself and everyone else.
13. I am enough, I have enough, I do enough.
14. I'm perfect just the way I am.
15. I am God's gift to the world.
16. I belong.
17. I have value.
18. I'm worth what I want.
19. I no longer have to earn the love I already deserve.
20. I know I am loved.

—7—

Clear the Decks

It was Thanksgiving Day when George moved into Martha's loft. He kept his own apartment on Thompson Street because, he rationalized, it was so cheap he couldn't afford to give it up. Martha wasn't thrilled with this arrangement, but it was better than nothing.

They were still wild about each other.

Martha cooked a fabulous turkey, which they didn't eat until midnight. They spent the whole day unpacking and making love. The sunset was primo. They sat on the terrace sipping white wine and kissing mouthfuls back and forth. Martha giggled and drooled wine all over her. George told her she shouldn't drink more than she could hold.

The next morning George woke up with a headache. He climbed out of bed, a gigantic king-sized water bed Martha and Philip had purchased, and drifted into the kitchen to make some coffee. He couldn't shake the headache until he remembered his weird dream about a man in a trench coat shooting him in the head. He took a deep breath, imagined the scene again, saw himself get up, after being shot, and run off. When he opened his eyes, the headache was gone.

He looked around the flat, which felt like anything but home. He especially despised all the photographs on the walls. How many dumb sunsets do you need? He began to feel like he was trapped in a Hallmark card.

He opened a closet and a man's trench coat greeted him. He slammed the door. Philip.

He looked at all the modular units in the living room, and it felt like plastic. Like *Town and Country* magazine. He hated magazines like that.

He noticed a photograph on a teak end table and picked it up. It was a picture of Martha in a black bikini somewhere in the Caribbean. Mexico, maybe. Cozumel. He turned the picture over and there was an inscription, "Forever, Philip!" George calmly took the picture out of the frame, turned on the gas stove and burned it. He dropped the flaming photograph into the sink and watched "forever" melt and disintegrate into black ash. "Forever, my ass!" he said to himself.

George had been to Martha's loft many times, but moving in opened his eyes to many things he had never noticed as a visitor.

He finished his coffee and went into the bathroom to shower and shave. When he opened the medicine cabinet, he noticed two Gillette razors, blades, Old Spice shaving cream, Brut deodorant, Grey Flannel cologne, and an old toothbrush. He calmly collected all these items and dumped them in the wastepaper basket.

He got dressed without shaving or showering and went out. He walked east on Bethune Street to Bleecker, where he sat down in a coffee shop and ordered a cappuccino. He wondered if he was making the biggest mistake of his life or whether this was all part of his dream coming true. It could go either way, he thought. Then he remembered my telling him there are no mistakes in life, only success and lessons, and once you learn the lessons, greater success followed; but if you run away from the lessons, they pursue you like your own shadow. God is very generous, I had said. He gives you infinite opportunities to learn the same lesson. At that moment, however, George felt more like shaking his own shadow than trusting God's teaching techniques.

He walked back to his flat on Thompson Street, where he shaved, showered, and lay down on his old dusty mattress on the floor. He fell asleep and dreamed about a big building on fire. When he woke up, he felt more himself, and he got dressed and went back to Martha's place.

That was the problem. It was still Martha's place. Even Martha and Philip's place. All that would have to change. The water bed would go. The photographs would go. The modular units, out! And whatever else it took. George knew he would not go. Martha was worth cleaning house for.

When he returned to Westbeth, Martha was awake and cooking omelettes. He snuggled up behind her and wrapped his arms around her long, languorous, naked body.

"I thought you moved out," she joked.

"No way. I'm here for the duration."

She swivelled around in his arms and looked him square in the eye.

"I know," she said. "I've got some past life stuff haunting this place."

"It's time to clear the decks, sweetheart."

WAY #7: CLEAR THE DECKS

If you don't want to leave, you have to make roots. In order to make roots you must clear a space, pull out weeds. Most of us live lives cluttered with remnants of the past, little mementos of old love we cling to as if they comprised our real identities. We tend to get addicted to nostalgia. Be it an old photograph, a piece of jewelry, furniture, or an article of clothing left behind, these objects haunt our space and actually chase new energy away.

Objects have thoughts, the thoughts and feelings of people who owned and touched them, and these thoughts are as powerful as the ones in our own minds. Old objects can drive an unconscious wedge between new lovers. It can be a painful process to sever old roots and clear ground for new ones. Pain itself is the effort it takes to cling to the past. Nostalgia is the sweet pain of loss. Who needs it?

Clear the decks! Start over. If you're starting a new relationship, or transforming an old one, changing the physical environment can nurture it more than you think. Redecorate your life. Don't sleep in your old bed, where old lovers have left their impression. Take a good conscious look at the physical world you've created and make the necessary adjustments to suit your new purpose and vision.

It would be a shame to lose a relationship because you found an old trench coat in the closet.

AFFIRMATIONS

1. *It's time for me to clear the decks.*

2. *It's easy to let go of the relics of past relationships.*

3. *My space is holy and I keep it clear.*

4. *I release all clutter from my life.*

5. *I leave my past behind me.*

6. *I don't need anything to remind me of what I'd prefer to forget.*

7. *Whatever I've lost is a blessing in disguise.*

8. *My vision for my future is more important than my pictures of the past.*

9. *Thank God I'm free of the past.*

10. *My space is a welcome space.*

11. *I am not threatened by my lover's past.*

12. *I never have to leave because of my partner's past.*

13. *My lover wants me more than the past.*

14. *I'm safe with ghosts.*

15. *I am no longer affected by anyone's past.*

16. *It's safe to stay and start over.*

17. *I belong in this relationship more than anyone else.*

18. *I have the right to make this relationship my home.*

19. *My presence itself cleanses any environment.*

20. *My presence dissolves the past.*

—8—

Stop the Movie, I Want to Get Out

George's head was going in circles. It wasn't drugs or alcohol, but it was definitely an altered state. The reason his mind was spinning was the conversation he was having with Martha.

"Why don't you get a straight job?" Martha had asked.

"I don't want to."

"Why don't you want to?"

"I don't want to want to!"

"Why don't you want to want to?"

"Beats the hell out of me."

This was the third time in the last fifteen minutes that they had gone around that particular circle. George was feeling swept away, out of his body, sucked into a vortex like Dorothy into the tornado. He wondered if he'd end up in a land like Oz and whether there'd be a powerless wizard and a wicked witch to confront. Or whether he'd just keep swimming around in circles forever.

Martha, for her part, was sure she was in a movie. An old movie. An old movie she had seen, seen again and re-run countless other times in her mind. It was not a very good movie. And the worst part of it was that she was stuck in the movie, playing a role that was so miserable she wished she could just crawl out from under its skin. If you had to stick a title on this particular film, and God knows why you'd want to, you could call it "L.A. Fantasy #9," or you could just leave it untitled and trash all the footage.

To fully understand and appreciate Martha's movie you'd have to go back in time to when her parents, Alex and Sarah, were her age, which would be 1931, long before she was even a twinkle in her father's eye. Long before Alex Kaplan was rich and famous. Long before his Beverly Hills mansion. In 1931, Alex and Sarah were living on the Lower East Side of Manhattan in a one bedroom walk-up on Clinton Street. Alex was a recent graduate of Columbia and wanted to do Shakespeare in New York. Sarah worked at Macy's supporting the two of them while he paced about their flat rehearsing soliloquies:

> There is a special providence in the fall of a sparrow;
> If it be now, it be not to come;
> If it be not to come, it be now,
> The readiness is all.

Sarah would climb up the three flights with two shopping bags in her arms, unlock the door, and discover him dueling a ghost or imaginary enemy. She thought he was gone. She was right. She sat down with him and urged him to give up his fantasy and get a straight job, or at least help her carry the groceries. She begged him night after night to come back to her. To be realistic. To have a little humility and get any little job. When the market crashed and the Depression hit, her begging turned to pleading and her pleading to commanding.

One day when he couldn't stand it any more, Alex Kaplan took off for Los Angeles. He left a note behind:

> My dearest Sarah,
>
> I received an offer I could not turn down. L.A. is calling and I am on my way. Will send for you soon. Please understand that this is not the end but the beginning.
>
> Realistically yours, Alex!

And it was a Hollywood ending. Alex made it as a director, then film producer, then went to law school and studied entertainment law at UCLA, and the rest is history. The day he summoned Sarah from Macy's, flew her to Los Angeles and showed her their new home in Beverly Hills, she forgave him forever and surrendered completely.

"Why don't you get a straight job?" she asked again.

"I don't want to."

"Why don't you want to?"

"I don't want to want to."

"Why don't you want to want to?"

"Beats the hell out of me."

How do you re-run a movie that was born before you were? How do you tap into parental behavior that previewed before you had eyes? Martha had no idea how this happened, nor did she care. She knew she was going over old reels, projecting on George for no logical reason. George, it was true, was unemployed, like Philip, like Alex twenty years before her conception. His role in the soap had been cancelled and he lost the 1776 part two weeks before opening. And it was also true that Martha would often come home from her job at McGraw-Hill to discover George rehearsing characters he would never play. Like Philip taking dumb pictures of sunsets, like Alex with his Shakespeare twenty years before she was a gleam in his eye. This was all true. But it was equally true that George had saved $50,000 and was going to get another job in his chosen field, and that what he was going through was an ordinary lull in any rising young star's orbit. She knew all this, but she couldn't help herself from carrying on the same dumb conversation. She was stuck in the movie, and she couldn't stop the projector.

So she threw George out of the loft and told him she never wanted to see him again.

Such is the power of an old movie.

George went back to Thompson Street totally bewildered. He had no idea what was going down. He loved Martha more than ever, knew she loved him equally, and had total faith in his career and their future together. Deep down inside he felt certain that this was a temporary crisis at worst, a lovers' misunderstanding, but he couldn't for the life of him understand what it was he misunderstood.

He gave me a call and explained the situation.

"Very interesting," I remarked.

"For you it's interesting, doc. For me it's crazy."

"Same difference."

"What do you mean?"

"We make our lives crazy so we can understand the craziness of our childhood. You're an actor, George. A born mimic. All kids are. We learn by imitating. On some unconscious level, you're re-creating an early event in your life.''

"Not again, doc?''

"Again and again, George, until you resolve the whole movie.''

"Shit.''

When George got off the phone, he lay down, breathed as he had learned to do, and let his mind furnish the missing scenes. He was so open it didn't take very long before he remembered a scene from his early years. It was in Honolulu. He couldn't have been more than two years old, but he could see the whole movie clear as day in living color and Dolby sound. His mother, Elizabeth, was angry at his new father. Frank Abrahms looked like James Cagney in George's memory bank. He was born to be a detective and that was exactly his dream. Elizabeth, however, thought that was stupid. Grown men were not private eyes. Frank tried to persuade her but she wouldn't come around. In the scene George was recalling, his mother was demanding that Frank get a straight job and help support the family. Frank was saying how he thought he'd go to L.A. and try to get something going there. Elizabeth was telling him that if he went to L.A., he shouldn't bother coming back. Frank replied that he didn't plan on coming back so much as moving them to L.A. Elizabeth threw her purse at Frank and told him to get out, she never wanted to see him again.

Of course, she did see him again. So did George. Because Frank Abrahms made it in L.A. in just six months, opening his "Red Eye Detective Agency" and doing what he loved to do, detect. They all lived in Hollywood for two years before Frank moved his whole operation to New York, where George grew up.

When George opened his eyes, he understood everything he had seen. All the pieces of the puzzle fit neatly into place.

When they came to me for a consultation, they were like two guilty puppies. George instantly apologized to Martha for giving her such a hard time. He told her why he had set up the whole situation. Martha, for her part, just laughed. She gave him a dozen long-stemmed roses and he cracked up. No woman had ever given him flowers. This was definitely not an old pattern. All he could say was:

"Let's go to the movies, huh?''

Way #8: Stop the Movie, I Want to Get Out

Our lives are like the movies. Ideally, we write the script, produce, direct, and star in the final version. But sometimes we don't seem to get the final edit.

And before we do, we seem to play supporting roles in other people's films, particularly our parents, our greatest role models. We win no Academy Awards for these supporting parts. We just tend to be unconscious witnesses to the drama of our parents' relationship. Then we take the stuff we witness and build our own movies on it.

We often project onto a current relationship whatever thoughts, feelings, and impressions are unresolved from our past. Even stuff that was unresolved in our parents' minds that we never actually witnessed. Unconsciously, we're trying to work out our past, or our parents' past, taking on their pain and projecting it onto our present lives for further clarification, as it were. This is called the Law of Projection and it is as powerful as your Primal Law.

A woman with a father who was a compulsive gambler sees her husband betting on a Monday night football game, and she freaks out. Even though he does it just once, maybe only wagering five dollars, she sees him through the memory of her dad's compulsion and overreacts as a result.

A man whose mother was an alcoholic sees his wife, an occasional drinker, sip a glass of wine, and he storms out of the room as though she has thrown her life to the devil. Behind his storm is all the pain, hurt, and fury towards his mother for drowning her life in alcohol.

The Law of Projection blinds us to present time reality. It causes many relationships to end when they don't have to. If you do not see the real reality of a situation, you react with the futility of a past reality you felt helpless to change and therefore shut down on.

Stop the projector! Climb out of the silver screen. You don't have to be in any movie you find hopeless. You can always go back to the editing room and cut the scenes from the past you no longer desire to project on your present, or future.

It's up to you! No one's making this movie but you.

AFFIRMATIONS

1. *I see the present for what it is.*

2. *Whenever I overreact, I see it as an opportunity to release past pain.*

3. *In present time there is no problem I cannot overcome.*

4. *I no longer project the past onto the present.*

5. *I forgive myself whenever I project the past onto the present.*

6. *My feelings are valid no matter where they come from.*

7. *Since my feelings are valid, even my projections are useful to my healing.*

8. *I never blame my partner for my projections.*

9. *I forgive myself for blaming my partner for my projections.*

10. *I forgive my partner for his/her projections.*

11. *I forgive my partner for blaming me for his/her projections.*

12. *I never leave a relationship as a result of a projection.*

13. *My vision is more powerful than my projections.*

14. *I am in charge of the movie of my life.*

15. *I choose to create my movie in my image, not my parents'.*

16. *I forgive myself for imitating my parents' negativity.*

17. *I forgive my parents for their pain.*

18. *I can love my parents without imitating them.*

19. *I only imitate my higher self.*

20. *God has the final edit on my life.*

—9—

Don't Take the Money and Run

The summer of '68 was a real scorcher, and one particular August day was the hottest in twenty-five years, and that's hot. George developed a rash around his neck, and Martha teased him about being all twisted up in the umbilical cord. George didn't think it was very funny. He developed a painful cough, too, even though he hadn't smoked since the day he met Martha.

He still didn't have a job and it was getting him down. Martha had been supporting him for five months now, and he hated being dependent. Even though he wasn't. He still had his $50,000 in a high interest account, but neither of them ever referred to it. He could see that Martha was beginning to resent providing for him, patterns or no patterns, even though she kept it to herself. It was obvious she didn't want to be the sole supporter. What Martha wanted was to quit her job and paint full time.

One night there was a blackout. They lit candles and the loft radiated romance. Martha put on her sexiest lingerie, and George forgot about money. They lay down on their new brass bed. Martha ran her long pink fingernails across her violet nylons and the sound alone almost made him come. She giggled. He reached for her breasts beneath her lilac teddy. As soon as he touched them, it happened. He started coughing uncontrollably and couldn't stop. Martha rolled him over and tried to help him, but he couldn't find his breath.

"I've got to get some air," he said, and sprang out of bed, got dressed, and went out. Martha was crushed. All her stuff about being undesirable came up. Plus she couldn't help him. Plus he didn't have a job. Plus he left. The total of all these pluses in Martha's mind was one big zero. "Men!" she cried. She sat on the bed and pulled her legs up, knees under her chin, and hugged herself. Tears streamed down her face. She loved George and it was killing her. Was this the end?

George felt much better once he was on the street. His cough subsided, he took some deep breaths and walked aimlessly. The Village was aglow in the blackout. Candles, lanterns, and kerosene lamps dotted Bleecker Street. The sky was exploding with stars you couldn't normally see. He walked to the Spring Street Bar in Soho and ordered a Bass Ale. He ran his hand around his neck and found his rash had disappeared. He chugged down one beer and ordered another. He wasn't coughing. He wondered if he was allergic to Martha? Or was it birth trauma? Both, he guessed.

He thought about his $50,000 and tried to imagine all that cash in one suitcase. He suddenly realized he was thinking about taking his money and running off to Hollywood to seek his fame and fortune. And it didn't feel like a pattern, it felt like, well, destiny. His agent had begun to discuss this possibility with George. There were no great prospects in New York this fall, an off-Broadway show and a couple of commercials, possibly, but nothing really exciting. George yearned to make it big. He was driven by the knowledge of his talent and his love of acting. He knew he had it in him to be a movie star, and he had no doubt he would eventually make it. He remembered all the encouragement his mother gave him. One day she had told him he would win an Academy Award and she helped him write his acceptance speech. He remembered the puppet shows he produced first for his mom, then his friends, then his entire elementary school. He remembered the first time he walked on a stage, playing the Captain in Gilbert and Sullivan's *H.M.S. Pinafore*. He could feel all the energy rush through his body as though he were there. After his performance his mom told him he was a star. She kept calling him her little star. So it seemed only natural that when he was looking for a stage name, he chose Starr.

George had a sudden impulse to call his agent. David Levy was not only an agent, but a friend. Recently divorced, David was hanging out with George and Martha quite a bit lately. They had met at NYU Drama School, where George was playing all the leads and David studying theater administration. They formed a business alliance shortly before graduation and both their careers had skyrocketed almost at once. David had landed George a good supporting role in a Neil Simon comedy, several commercials, and numerous parts at Joseph Papp's Public Theater. David was now 26 and considered one of the best independent agents in the city.

He had good news for George. There was a leading role available in the new John Walker movie being shot in L.A. Filming started in three weeks and he'd have to decide soon. David asked how Martha would like the idea. George wanted to read the script.

He picked it up that night, went back to Thompson Street, called Martha, and told her he needed some time alone, and spent twenty-four hours reading the most god-awful screenplay ever written, he was sure. It was a dumb comedy about a Mexican invasion of the United States. George would play a Mexican bandit who looked American and who seduced the first female Vice President, married her and then assassinated the President and took over. The script was a poor imitation of a bad Mel Brooks movie, complete with musical duds, such as "Mexico, the Beautiful!"

Yes, it was a leading role, but leading where? George lay on his old dusty mattress and tried to put the last week in perspective.

He felt all his leaving energy propelled by his thoughts of having to make it on his own. He thought about his greedy desire to take the money and run. He thought about L.A. and how it pulled at him from somewhere deep in his soul. And he thought about Martha and how she pulled at him from an even deeper place.

He closed his eyes and saw her as he had left her the night before. He could see her scratching her nylons and it turned him on. Who was this woman whom he loved so very much? Whom he could not leave. Who was still a total mystery to him. Her exquisite physical beauty was but the outer shell, and between the surface and the core seemed an infinite number of other layers. She was like an onion it would take eternity to peel.

Martha was home at the time, painting and also thinking. She knew George would come back, but she wanted to be clear on the money thing. She realized that what she wanted the most was to quit her job and paint, and for George to support them with his $50,000. She understood that the reason she had been unable to ask for what she most wanted was because her father had lost that $50,000 at her birth, and she always felt she owed men money. She could see how that affected her relationships with both Philip and George. Maybe, subconsciously, she had always held men back from success because she secretly felt unworthy of receiving from them. She felt too guilty to be supported as a woman.

George got dressed and walked back home to Westbeth. When he opened the door, Martha was painting an oil of the blackout. She looked up at him as he closed the door behind him.

"So," she said, "are you leaving?"

"No. I'm not leaving. You are. You're leaving your job tomorrow."

WAY #9: DON'T TAKE THE MONEY AND RUN

Money is the last refuge of the ego. It represents survival, and when survival and surrender bang heads against each other, all hell breaks loose.

Usually, when two people fall, or rise, in love and get together, they each have their separate resources, jobs, savings, maybe investments they bring into the relationship. While it might not be the wisest thing in the world to pool all these resources at once, there comes a time for every couple when they have to look at this issue.

When you are committed to a loving relationship, you are pulled to an experience of greater and greater oneness, perhaps a sense of the spiritual unity behind all apparent diversity. The more this pull grabs you, the more you are called upon to let go of every piece of separation you have imposed on your spirit. You cannot be one and separate at the same time. In love you find that the more you cling to separation, the more cut off from yourself you become.

Love drives us to be whole, but we are addicted to making it on our own. And money, more than anything else, represents our success at separate survival. It is therefore natural that we are tempted to keep separate savings and checking accounts, to share equally but not wholly in our finances. No one wants to be ripped off. Especially if one partner has more money than the other.

But love is based on trust and faith, while money often seems based on mistrust and suspicion. The choice is simple. Do you reduce love to the ego's world of calculation and measurement, or do you transform your relationship to money so that it is aligned with the spiritual world of love?

Ultimately, the more you pool your money, the more money the pool provides for you. But no intelligent capitalist would tell you this.

Affirmations

1. *I always have more than enough money.*
2. *Love increases my wealth.*
3. *It's safe to share.*
4. *The more I give, the more I have.*
5. *Whatever I give comes back to me multiplied.*
6. *My desire to give is greater than my fear of running out.*
7. *I am surrounded by wealth.*
8. *I always have my fair share coming to me.*
9. *I deserve to receive.*
10. *I'm worthy of wealth.*
11. *My partner loves me for who I am, not what I possess.*
12. *People love to give to me.*
13. *People only give to me freely.*
14. *I never feel obligated by receiving.*
15. *It's fun to provide for my partner.*
16. *It's fun to be provided for.*
17. *God provides for all our needs.*
18. *Surrendering to love generates abundance.*
19. *We are a money magnet.*
20. *Money comes to us from unexpected sources.*

— 10 —

If You Must Get on the Bus, Gus . . .

Martha quit her job the next day. George took her shopping for art supplies and spent $1000 on paints, brushes, palettes, easels, canvas, and enrolling her in a drawing class at The New School. It was one of their best days ever. They had lunch at The Buffalo Roadhouse and dinner at El Faros, and made love all night, and then again at dawn.

George felt a new power emerge from his choice to support Martha. He adored watching her paint. She would lose herself in her colors and forms much like an actor in a character, and the way her body moved with a paintbrush reminded him of Judith Jamison of the Alvin Ailey Ballet.

George read scripts. He was getting offers. David Levy was kicking ass for him. He did a commercial for Chemical Bank where the chemistry was right, agreed to play Richard III at the Public Theater and had several screen tests for New York-based movies. October was his favorite month. Two weeks before rehearsals for Richard began, they rented a car and drove through New England, where Martha painted 10,000 autumn leaves, and George learned his Shakespeare. She loved him when he got into the flesh of a character the way he did with Richard. His whole body took on the twisted fate of the wretched king. One night he made love to her as the cripple, and she couldn't stop coming, or laughing. Her appetite for sex kept increasing, it seemed to George. The more they satisfied each other, the more their passion blossomed. There was no end to their energy. They hardly even slept because they seemed to be in a state of constant renewal. Sleep felt like a waste of time.

She remained a complete mystery to him. The more he knew her, the less he seemed to understand and the more he felt compelled to explore. The more he was enchanted with her, the more enchantment she felt. She seemed, to herself, to be a woman for the first time, an amorphous feeling entity, a rapidly growing organism, like a giant amoeba reaching, spreading and extending herself throughout the universe. None of this made sense to her rational mind, but she could not deny the feelings. She tried to paint what she felt, but her art had not yet caught up with her soul. She accepted this lag time as necessary, and continued to paint leaves.

They returned to New York early in November and it was unseasonably cold, raw, bitter. Snow flurries were whirling about. George buried himself in Richard III for which he got rave notices but no new intriguing offers. David Levy was again talking about the West Coast. By Christmas they had spent a good deal of money. George bought her a black mink coat and diamond earrings for the holidays, and she, in turn, gave him a fabulous leather jacket and boots. David came over for Christmas dinner and couldn't stop talking about L.A., where he had just been.

"It's eighty degrees out there. The fruit is incredible. And the opportunities, George, they're begging for you out there."

"What have you got?"

"Well, nothing certain. You gotta be there. Arthur Penn's auditioning, Brian de Palma's interested and Mike Nichols asked specifically for you. Look. I'm thinking of moving out there myself next month. I've had it with winter."

New Year's came and went, and the snow piled up, as did the bills. They spent their days mostly in silence, happy, content, but each of them thinking about what David had said.

One day George was daydreaming about Hollywood. He was imagining his Academy Award speech, as he had rehearsed it with his mom. He drifted in and out of consciousness. He saw himself getting on a Greyhound bus bound for L.A. He was waving goodbye to Martha, who was very pregnant and crying. He was telling her he'd send for her, and he remembered thinking he was acting like his dad again. Who was his dad anyway? There was his real dad and his fake dad, Frank, who was his real dad. That was another mystery he'd have to solve. Another movie. After Martha. Suddenly, he was on a bus full of soldiers and

David Levy was driving. David smiled and told the soldiers it was their job to save Hollywood from the Mexican invasion.

"It's a lousy job, but someone's got to do it!"

George was mumbling in his daydream. Martha was painting. For some reason she didn't understand she was painting a big Greyhound bus driving through the desert. It was like a Georgia O'Keeffe desert, full of mystery and whimsy, an ancient place of deep unknown messages. And this big mother of a bus slicing through. At the last minute she painted L.A. on the bus's destination sign.

Then she stopped. She impulsively knew what she must do. She woke up George and told him to start packing, they were taking a bus to L.A.

"Together?" he mumbled.

"Of course together. You think I'd let you go alone?"

WAY #10:
IF YOU MUST GET ON THE BUS, GUS . . .

Many couples create unnecessary separation over where to live or work. You can unconsciously create a job opportunity far away from your home if your leaving pattern is up. Or you can create your partner creating such an opportunity if your abandonment pattern is up. Always something!

Many couples fight furiously over where to live. East Coast or West? North or south? City or country? These are false fights because the real issue is psychology, not geography. If you're in a leaving frame of mind, there are 10,000 ways to play out the scenario. Any minor disagreement could erupt into a major cataclysm threatening the whole relationship.

The solution is simple. Go where your partner goes. Whoever has the strongest pull to go somewhere is the leader at that point in the relationship. It is not a compromise to follow the one you love to the end of the earth when you know, in your heart, he, or she, will lead you further to yourself, not to mention the adventure of the journey.

Remember, your choice to be one requires give and take, flexibility. Usually, when you are most stubborn on this type of issue is when you are clinging to nothing for no good reason. Such is the power of sepa-

ration. Ultimately, your relationship is your mobile home anyway, your Greyhound, your vehicle. So get on the bus with Gus, and leave the driving to whoever is in the driver's seat.

Affirmations

1. My first priority is my relationship.
2. I'd rather be with my mate than anywhere else.
3. Home is where my heart is.
4. I never need to leave love in order to find work.
5. I no longer have to be separate to survive.
6. I love to travel with my partner.
7. It's fun to explore new places together.
8. I'd rather let go and move on than hold on and be stubborn.
9. I can be grounded on the move.
10. I can feel at home most anywhere.
11. The Earth is my home; I am a global citizen.
12. My relationship guides me to appropriate living spaces.
13. I can always go back.
14. I never lose when I move on.
15. Every move I make gives me more of what I want.
16. Moving is easy and pleasurable.
17. My partner and I move in harmony.
18. The more I support my partner in his/her moves, the more supported I feel in mine.
19. I no longer re-create my birth scenario when I move.
20. God made me mobile so I'm free to move.

—11—

Forgive and Forget

The real reason Martha had resisted L.A. was that her family lived there, and she had avoided them like the plague for five years, ever since her dad called Philip a bum. She hated it when her dad was right. It made her feel all wrong again.

So when she decided to go with George, she knew she was also choosing to go home and make her peace. On the bus she had plenty of time to think. She remembered her mom telling her how she didn't want to leave New York and that the only reason she had gone was her dad was so adamant. Patterns, patterns. Martha's mom had never really become a California person. Being rich had eased the pain but, in her heart, Sarah Kaplan would always be a New Yorker. Martha wondered if she could do what her mom could not. In the past she had thought of her mom as weak and sacrificing. Now that she was wearing the same shoes, she didn't know. She felt a new respect for her mom for following her man. Tears welled up inside her. She realized how much she had cut herself off from her family and their love for her. The cost of separation was no longer worth the price. And she no longer had any desire to be cut off from anyone she loved. Except her dad. But she didn't love him. Or did she love him most of all? She didn't know.

George was also thinking of Martha's dad. He knew she would have to make her peace with him in order for their relationship to continue to flourish. He remembered what I had told them both, that anything unresolved with their parents would come up in their relationship for healing. He also remembered what his mother had taught him, never to marry a woman who didn't have a good relationship with her father. George believed both these statements, and he had, in part, wanted to move to L.A. to stir things up between Martha and her dad. Stirring being a positive action, he prayed. In fact, he had spent all his money except for $1000, paying rent for both Thompson Street and Westbeth for a year, in case they decided to move back, as well as deposit and security on a small lovely house on the beach in Malibu, which David Levy had found for them.

George knew they'd have to borrow money from Martha's father. He also knew that it was the last thing in the world she wanted to do. As he sat on the bus watching the desert roll by, George was relishing the inevitable drama that would go down. He was an actor first and foremost, but once in a while he loved to play the director.

Martha was asleep on his shoulder. If she had been awake she would have noticed her painting outside the window, the Georgia O'Keeffe mystery with the bus slicing through. But she was dreaming at the time, envisioning a tearful reunion with her father, smelling his cigar, feeling his strong arms holding her. George noticed she was weeping in her sleep, whimpering and crying, "Daddy, Daddy."

Things did not turn out the way George planned. They turned out better. When they arrived at their house in Malibu and settled in, George told Martha their financial situation was a bit precarious and *she* suggested they borrow money from her dad.

"It will be a good opportunity to heal my relationship with him." George couldn't believe he was hearing the words.

Martha had worked it all out in her mind. Her ability to surrender to George's $50,000 had somehow cleared the karmic debt. She saw things differently now. First of all, she knew she was worthy as a woman or George wouldn't love her so much. One thing George had was excellent taste. Secondly, it was now okay with her that her father had wanted a boy. Now that she accepted herself as a woman, she could accept her father as a typical man, wanting a son for his firstborn. His intuition wasn't so hot, she thought, but she guessed he had paid for that. $50,000. Plus her resentment, which she knew hurt him. But now she saw it all in a new light. She didn't know if she had forgiven him. Suddenly, there seemed to be nothing to forgive.

She also was able to see how much her dad loved her. Her resentment had blinded her to all the good times they had, but in letting go she remembered sitting on his lap, his hugs, his warmth, the long walks on the beach, and his teaching her to ride her first bicycle when he couldn't ride one himself. All the suppressed fond memories came pouring through.

Poor Dad, she thought, stuck with three daughters. King Lear himself. And when she reminded herself that one of her younger sisters was gay and the other bisexual, she felt nothing but compassion for her dad.

When they visited her parents, George spent a lot of time in the jacuzzi with her mom, discussing the movie industry, Martha, and her sisters. Meanwhile Martha and her dad walked out by the pool.

"Just like old times, eh?" Alex Kaplan asked tentatively.

"Yeah, Dad."

"I've missed you, baby."

"Oh God, I missed you too, Daddy."

They dissolved into tears. They hugged. They laughed as they shared old memories. And he wouldn't hear of loaning them money. He gave her $10,000 and told George to take care of his precious angel.

"You know, when she was born, I wanted a boy."

"So I heard."

"I even made a small wager on her sex."

"Heard that, too."

"It was a dumb thing to do, but I got over it. The fact is, the moment I saw her blue eyes I knew she was worth every penny I lost."

WAY #11: FORGIVE AND FORGET

Your parents did the best they could. That's the bottom line, and everything else amounts to nothing.

The point at which you cut off from one or both of your parents is the point at which you inevitably cut off from your present partner. If you really want to surpass your parents, which would only delight them, you must forgive them first.

Forgiveness is not thinking they were bad and then condescending to spare them your wrath. That's a demeaning approach to forgiveness. In its higher form, forgiving is seeing that there was no wrongdoing in the first place, just negative thoughts in their minds and yours which collided. Many good people act bad because they had bad thoughts.

You've done it yourself a few times. Forgiving your parents is releasing your judgements on them and yourself. It sets you free. Forgiveness therefore is its own reward, especially when you think of all the pain and illness that carrying resentment in your body can cause. Besides, deep in your heart, you've always loved your parents and they you. Yes, they've seemed to hurt you. And you them. But now you're strong enough to release old pain and go for the highest thought, namely that there was no wrongdoing, only wrongthinking.

See your parents in a new light and that light will shed grace on your whole life. Your parents must have done a few things right or else you would not have turned out so wonderful yourself. In forgiving them your self-esteem automatically takes a leap.

We have so much to be thankful to our parents for. Let's forget the rest.

Affirmations

1. *I forgive my father completely.*

2. *I forgive my mother completely.*

3. *I forgive myself completely.*

4. *I dwell in gratitude, not regret.*

5. *All my resentments dissolve into gratitude.*

6. *I am willing to see my parents in a new light.*

7. *I now view the past from my present contentment.*

8. *I am no longer limited by my parents' limiting thoughts.*

9. *I can surpass my parents without rejecting them.*

10. *I am grateful to my parents.*

11. *On some level I know I chose my parents and they me.*

12. *I thank God for all I learned from my parents.*

13. *I no longer separate myself from my parents in order to be myself.*

14. *I can be myself in a family.*

15. *I no longer hold my parents in negative thoughts.*

16. *The more I grow, the more my parents grow.*

17. *My parents are perfect just the way they are.*

18. *I can disagree with my parents and still love them.*

19. *I set my parents free.*

20. *I thank my parents for having me.*

—12—

Shake the Blues

Martha came down with a bad case of the blues. Maybe she was listening to too much Janis Joplin. Maybe she missed New York more than she admitted. Maybe it was something else.

David Levy noticed it first. It was late June, 1969. He attributed her moodiness to Bobby Kennedy's assassination and Vietnam. This was a rather obvious conclusion since he noticed she painted ten portraits of Kennedy, all in blue. And that all her other recent paintings were entirely blue as well. He had heard of Picasso's blue period, but Martha's was beginning to look like a more permanent point of view. Even her face had a bluish hue these days. He even told her so.

"Funny, you don't look bluish," she responded.

David loved Martha's face. To him it was a mixture of Faye Dunaway's royalty and Doris Day's homespun cuteness. It was cold and it was warm at the same time and, depending on her mood, one or the other would define her expression. These days, however, Martha looked lukewarm, and David, being a friend, was concerned.

George was off on a shoot in Mexico. He had landed his first meaty part in a film. No, not another cheap Mel Brooks imitation. This one was called *Temple*, and George played a British missionary who falls in love with a Mayan priestess. The film never went anywhere, but George's performance would launch his career once and for all.

Martha missed George, who had been gone for three weeks. But the source of her despair was old, not new. She invited David over for dinner, and he brought it up over the soufflé.

"Are you a hopeless romantic, Martha?"

"I guess, David."

"The L.A. blues got a hold of you?"

"Could be."

"I was just wondering."

"Wondering what?"

"If all artists are hopelessly romantic. By romantic, I don't mean romance. Romance is hot, red, yellow, bright greens. Romantic is dark, lugubrious, like a morbid fascination with futility."

"You think?"

"I do. Romance is life. Romantic is death. Look at all the great romantic lovers. Romeo and Juliet. Morbid stuff. Is that your vision?"

"Absolutely not."

"All these blue paintings, you know. They're excellent. Technically, they are quite fine. But it hurts like hell to look at them."

"It hurts to paint them."

"Why do you do it?"

"I can't help it."

"It concerns me, though. I guess I feel that what you paint is what you get. You know what I'm saying? Like if you see blue in your mind you live a blue life."

"I don't know."

"I do though. I had this client who played three parts where he was shot in the back. One day he was out in the woods and a complete stranger shot him in the back by mistake. One of those so-called hunting accidents."

"Jesus."

"I had another actress who kept getting divorced on stage. The next thing she knew she divorced and remarried her husband three times."

"That's weird."

"You gotta shake them blues, Martha."

She turned to look at all her Bobby Kennedy paintings.

"He was such a beautiful man."

"Paint his beauty, not his tragedy."

"I'm not sure I can separate them.."

"Sure you can. All you gotta do is separate yourself from your own gloom and doom."

"Maybe."

"Where's all that spunkiness you used to have?"

"I guess it's the times."

"Forget that. You're not a victim of the times. If it weren't the 60s, it'd be the 50s. What a bore they were. Or there's the 40s and the war and the 30s and the depression. There's always a good excuse for despair."

"I guess so."

"You miss George?"

"It's funny. I do and I don't. I mean, I miss his body like crazy. But the rest of him is with me, you know what I mean?"

"That's beautiful."

"You know, George was a blue baby. I wonder if I've taken that on in some bizarre way."

"That's another thing. I think you're both too stuck on this birth stuff. Don't you think it's time you put that behind you?"

Way #12: Shake the Blues

We all get moody once in a while, and there's no harm in it. Maybe it's the moon, the stars, biorhythms or the condition of our world. Maybe something else. The blues, however, can cause you to become preoccupied with loss, grief, and separation, and the more you dwell thereon, the more you build your world around it.

What is a mood but a lingering feeling with which you have a morbid fascination? You might be in love with the blues because it seems to make you feel more deeply, makes you more romantic, artistic, socially conscious. You can weep for the world soul if you want. Big deal. The world soul doesn't need your tears. It needs your cheers.

You have the power to change your moods. It's as simple as changing your mind. Since a bad mood tends to color everything blue, locating and releasing the thoughts responsible for the mood and replacing them with more life-affirming thoughts will change your whole world, lift your spirit and bring a rainbow of color back into your eyes.

For your relationship to grow, you must be an optimist. If you are a pessimist about life in general, you will create tragedy in your personal life. It's fine to have compassion for all the suffering in the world, but don't let your compassion get you down. Let it inspire you to help make a better world. You can let go of the blues without looking at the world through rose-colored glasses.

Take in all the colors of life. When you're blinded by the darkness how can you expect to see the light?

Shake them blues away!

Affirmations

1. *I am an optimist at heart.*
2. *I don't have to suffer to be creative.*
3. *I am innocent; I don't have to take on the pain of the world.*
4. *I can love without suffering for those I love.*
5. *I let go of past pain easily and quickly.*
6. *I am more fascinated with life than with death.*
7. *I choose joy and aliveness.*
8. *I am no longer a victim of mood swings.*
9. *I choose a good mood daily.*
10. *I have more to smile about than cry about.*
11. *I choose to look at the bright side of things.*
12. *I have every reason to celebrate life.*
13. *It's safe to rejoice.*
14. *My life is full of wonderful delights.*
15. *Every day I witness new miracles.*
16. *Other people are not my problem.*
17. *My happiness is my greatest gift to others.*
18. *I am an inspiration.*
19. *I love my life and show it.*
20. *I am too happy for the blues.*

—13—

Celebrate the Good Times

Alex Kaplan loved to celebrate success. His success, his wife's success, his daughters' success, anyone's success. He was what you might call a success-conscious individual. His philosophy was quite simple: celebrate the good times; to hell with the rest.

When George's movie, *Temple*, came out, Alex thumbed through all the papers and gathered the rave reviews (for George, not the movie), and he was so proud he read them aloud to his whole office staff one morning. Then he threw a huge bash at his mansion. George was fast becoming Alex's missing son. Martha didn't mind one bit. Why should she? It took the pressure off her.

Alex and George were walking poolside, Alex's arm slung fatherly over George's shoulder while he smoked his favorite Havana cigar with the other.

"I am so proud of you, boy. I really am."

"Thanks, Alex."

"Celebrate the good times, son."

"Why not?" George clanked his champagne glass against Alex's. They drank up.

"The more you celebrate success, the more success you get to celebrate."

"I'll buy that."

They returned to the party. David and Martha were dancing cheek to cheek. Martha's youngest sister, Karen, stole George's arm from her dad and danced with him, a little too closely. A live band was playing "Hey, Jude." The champagne and caviar were flowing freely. All the big movie stars were present—Hoffman, Newman, Fonda, and Beatty; Eastwood, Taylor, Lemmon, and Curtis. You just had to look around the place to know the kind of respect Alex Kaplan commanded in Hollywood. The band started playing, "Let the Good Times Roll," and George slithered out of Karen's grasp and looked for Martha, who was still dancing with David.

George took a deep breath, letting himself feel the exhilaration of success. He really liked Alex, who he knew would part the Red Sea for him. But he loved the guy too much to ask. Besides, he didn't need any miracles. They were already happening.

Karen whispered in his ear:

"How does it feel?"

"What?"

"To be one of the beautiful people?"

"I'm not quite sure."

"Oh, a snob are we?"

"I hope not."

"A sexy snob," she said, biting his ear.

"A monogamous snob," he added and pulled away for a second time.

Karen was twenty-two, a more Mediterranean beauty than Martha's Nordic perfection. Karen was obviously confused about her sexuality, had tried being gay like Sally, the middle sister, thought of herself as bisexual and was, basically, an incorrigible flirt. Much as George knew all this, he found himself inexplicably attracted to her.

David, meanwhile, held Martha close to him as the band played "Norwegian Wood."

"Is this what the good times feel like, David?"

"This is the real thing, baby." She couldn't stop laughing. She had had a little too much champagne.

"What's the joke?" he asked.

"It's just a party, and everyone's happy."

"You want more?"

"Oh, my God," Martha laughed again. "This is definitely L.A. What *am* I doing here?"

"In New York they'd say you were escaping reality."

"Is that why I feel so free?"

"Either that or the champagne."

"If this ain't reality, David, I question the need to look further."
They embraced as she burped.

George was watching while Alex was telling him,

"It's okay to get high if you got your feet on the ground."

"As long as you don't step on anyone getting there," George added.

"I'd like to give you a boost, son. I mean, I could really put you in
orbit now."

"One step at a time, Alex. Let me enjoy this peak for a while before
I notice I'm still in the foothills."

"I'm not putting you down, son." Alex puffed on his cigar.

"I know, Alex. I really appreciate all this."

Suddenly, tears came to Alex's eyes.

"I love my Martha, George."

"I'll drink to that, Alex," and they did.

"God bless you all," someone shouted and the band played the Beach
Boys hit, "Surfing, USA."

George was thinking, "Am I completely nuts, or is this just another
perfect day in paradise?"

A voice in his head replied, "You're completely nuts."

George and Martha were walking out by the pool, arm in arm. Suddenly, she turned and kissed him urgently. The moon was full. A gentle
breeze sighed in the eucalyptus trees. He held her to him.

"Let's get out of here," she whispered.

"You mean, go home?"

"I mean go, split, leave. What are we doing here?"

"Making it, baby, making it." He was kissing her neck the way he
knew she liked.

"Don't, George. Not here, not now."

"Here, baby. Now."

WAY #13: CELEBRATE THE GOOD TIMES

*The more you celebrate the good times, the more they roll. On and on
and on.*

*What is success? It's different for everyone. We all have our own
goals and aspirations, our own edition of the American dream. But*

whatever our pictures, we all anticipate a certain feeling at the moment of making it. And since the moment is so fleeting and doomed to fade, you either seize it when you get it, or it's gone before you know you had it.

Most people, when they attain a goal, hardly stop to acknowledge it or themselves. They simply move on to some new pursuit and begin the struggle to make it all over again. The result is they never really feel successful. They're too busy seeking something new. What a waste!

What's the point in climbing a mountain if you just walk back down once you're up there? Stop for a while. Take pause. Take it all in—what you've done, where you've come from, the view. Turn your moment of accomplishment into a peak experience.

No matter how big or small the goal is, when you reach it, celebrate it. Let it vibrate in the cells of your body. Dance to it. Sing to it. Let it sink into your mind. And share it with those you love. This way you build a success consciousness which generates greater and greater success. Besides, you've earned the pleasure.

Maybe, in the end, success has little to do with making it and more to do with a deep sense of spiritual well-being. Maybe we get too caught up in the material world's opinion of success. Maybe the American dream is, after all, gaudy, trashy, sleazy and tawdry.

So what? If you're walking through a dream, keep on going. If you're making it in tinseltown and tickertape, enjoy it. Celebrate the dream. When you wake up, you can deal with that other reality.

Don't run away from your dreams. Your heart's desires are always guiding you, not misleading you. You don't want to be one of those people who denies his dreams, stuffs his ambition and then pretends he's holier than thou. Go through the illusion on the path to truth.

And don't rain on your own parade!

AFFIRMATIONS

1. *I deserve all my successes.*

2. *I deserve to enjoy all my successes.*

3. *I love to share my success.*

4. *My success inspires others.*

5. *My success is innocent.*

6. *It's safe to celebrate my success.*

7. *It's safe to be more successful than others.*

8. *It's safe to surpass myself and show it.*

9. *I celebrate whenever I surpass myself.*

10. *When I am celebrating, I am thanking God.*

11. *People love to share my success.*

12. *People support my success.*

13. *I show off my success without ego.*

14. *I'd rather celebrate than struggle.*

15. *I never hide the success I attain.*

16. *It's good luck to celebrate success.*

17. *I never deny the success God sends my way.*

18. *The more I seize the moment, the more I succeed.*

19. *The more I celebrate, the more I seize the moment.*

20. *My success opens me more and more.*

—14—

Your Life Urge—Don't Leave Home Without It

George was on Cloud Nine. So what if *Temple* had bombed at the box office? He had been noticed and acclaimed. Plus he now had $75,000 in savings and stocks. Plus he had more new offers coming in than he could keep up with. He was hot. David Levy had to hire a new assistant just to keep up with requests for George. They were offering him the world—T.V., film, Broadway, you name it.

He started smoking a lot of dope. He started drinking a lot of tequila. He started smoking Camels. He bought a new red Corvette and drove too fast. He was definitely living life in the fast lane, fully launched, in orbit. His feet were nowhere near the ground.

Martha saw everything and said nothing. At first, she just said to herself that it was only a phase, he'd come out of it. Then she went into her brooding. Then her pouting. On the heels of which came sulking. She painted darker and darker shadows. The blues were gone. She was in her black period.

In October they drifted further and further apart. Martha kept dreaming about death, her own death. She saw herself dying in flaming plane crashes, car collisions, hanging from a tree, strapped to an electric chair, jumping off cliffs, nailed to a cross, drowning. Whatever. She died a thousand deaths that October.

Unknown to her conscious mind, Martha was working out her unconscious death urge. She wore only black. She bought a black Siamese cat. She hated the sun, or any light, and would sit in the dark for hours, shades drawn, ruminating. If a shaft of light shined anywhere, she ran to cover it.

George couldn't get near her. One night he came home late after drinking with some buddies. It was pitch black and she was sitting in her rocker with her cat, Noir, on her lap, rocking aimlessly. George turned on a light and she shrieked hysterically, as Noir scampered off to the closest dark corner, which happened to be outside the door George had left open. Martha started to dash off after her cat, for a moment showing a sign of activity, but when the light outside hit her eyes, she turned around and skulked off to the bedroom, weeping inconsolably. George tried to calm her down, but she pushed him away. In his frustration he slapped her across the face. Not hard. But still, a slap. She sat down on the bed, frozen in shock. She became catatonic. He tried to apologize, but she didn't even hear him. She heard nothing. He started weeping, but she didn't notice. Finally, he stormed out and flew off in his red Corvette.

Morning came but George didn't come home. The phone rang and Martha walked to it like a mummy. She picked up the receiver and it was her father. He had bad news. Her mother had cancer. Martha felt nothing.

George just wanted to die. He just wanted to dissolve like the Wicked Witch of the West into a bucket of water. Unknown to him, his father had died twenty-seven years ago that day, at age twenty-seven, which was exactly George's age. But George wasn't looking at his family tree. He was looking at losing Martha. He should have been looking at the road. All he kept thinking was fuck the world, fuck Hollywood, fuck, fuck, fuck!

He was winning the world and losing the universe. Fuck, fuck, fuck! He had a hot car but nowhere to go. Fuck, fuck, fuck! He was an idol, a star, a sex symbol to everyone except the only one that mattered. Fuck! He could feel his love for Martha pulling him apart, tearing at his guts, ripping his heart in two. He drove faster and faster away from her. He was pushing 85 MPH.

If he couldn't have perfection, he'd have nothing. Nothing. Fuck, fuck, fuck! 95 MPH! He was sobbing and shaking as he stepped down another notch on the accelerator. "Fuck it! Fuck it!" he screamed at the top of his lungs. 100 MPH! He saw himself slap her. And in his mind he hit her over and over again until she fell, a bloody mess onto their brass bed. Why he imagined destroying what he most loved he did not know. He just wanted to die and to kill her because . . . 110 MPH! He thought he had the answer when he heard the siren behind him. He turned around to look and never saw the black Mercedes 350 SEL cutting in front of him, nor the eighteen-year-old boy who was driving, his unconscious death urge also screaming for attention.

When Martha came to the hospital, George was in traction. Broken legs, arms, ribs, neck, jaw, concussion, lacerations, and bruises. Some internal bleeding. The doctor said it was a miracle that he was still alive. He told Martha George was very lucky, much luckier than the eighteen-year-old boy who was critical and whose family was praying for him. Martha felt nothing. She walked into his room and looked at him all wrapped up in bandages, legs up in the air. She almost envied him. He was unconscious. So was she. She put a dozen long-stemmed roses by his bed. She left.

She went to see her mom who was being very courageous. She was going to have a mastectomy, but she'd be okay. Or so she said. Alex said that one boob on mom was better than two on most women. Bad joke. Karen was crying and Sally, the middle sister, was trying to comfort her. Sally's girlfriend, Beth, was cooking ham and eggs. Martha was numb, her head in a fog. It was all a big blur to her.

Her dad insisted on driving her home. She said nothing about George's accident. She said nothing.

"You look like hell, baby."

She didn't respond.

"Wanna talk about it?"

Nothing.

"A time for laughter, a time for tears, huh? Ecclesiastes, I think." He puffed away at his Havana.

Martha noticed one of those huge Hollywood billboards. There was an ad for a Charles Bronson movie, *Death Wish*. She smiled.

"This isn't the end, kid. You know how I know? The end is always happy. This is Hollywood."

Alex dropped his daughter off, but she wouldn't let him in. She entered her dark home and noticed she had left one curtain open. She shut it. She could hear kids playing volleyball on the beach. She shut it out.

She was looking for Noir, her cat, wondering if he had come home. He was nowhere. She ended up in the bedroom and noticed it right away. In the middle of the bed. On the white bedspread. Noir. Asleep. She moved closer. Then she noticed the red stains on the white cover. And the tiny black body not breathing. Dead. Hit by a car. Crawled back to bed to die.

Martha clutched the dead cat to her bosom, stroking and rocking it. She could feel it all now, and the tears spurted from her eyes like geysers.

"Oh, Mom!" she cried. "Oh, George! Oh, God!"

WAY #14: YOUR LIFE URGE— DON'T LEAVE HOME WITHOUT IT

The unconscious death urge can drive a wedge in any relationship. When you reach the age when one of your parents died, or when one of your parents is dying, shock waves reverberate through your entire life. Or can.

> You can be depressed and gloomy for no apparent reason.
>
> Your plants can die.
>
> Your pets, too.
>
> Your car might not start.
>
> Your business might fail.
>
> Or your health.
>
> And your relationship can be driven to the brink.
>
> You can start to think:
>
> What's the point?
>
> What difference does it make?
>
> What does it matter anyway?
>
> Who the fuck cares?

The unconscious death urge is our unconscious choice to die. Most people think death is inevitable, hardly a matter of choice. But the single most powerful force that sustains our lives is the will to live. We all have a strong life urge or we would not be here in the first place, let alone have survived what we have gone through.

Your desire to live is greater than your desire to die, or you wouldn't be here reading this book.

But there are times when your will to live weakens, when you want to give up, feel life isn't worth the struggle or feel trapped in a closed system you want to break out of. There are times when life seems very limiting and death looks like a viable alternative, when you cannot surrender in the body and look for peace of another dimension. When your mind's in a downwards spiral, and your body hurts so much you want to climb out. Times when your death urge is up.

If you learn to recognize the signs, you can watch them go by without acting upon them. If you relax into an immortalist's context, you can have the magnitude of vision to allow your fear of and/or desire for death to leave your mind and body without actually doing yourself in. All death is suicide, in a manner of speaking, in the sense that death is a choice you make on some level when life ceases to be attractive enough to sustain.

It is eminently practical to see your life from the perspective of a continuum. You can begin to let go of the notion of a birth/death cycle, a closed belief system that brainwashes us into believing that everything has a beginning, middle, and end. If you enter love with the thought of built-in obsolescence, your days of joy and aliveness are numbered from the start. You're loving on borrowed time, as it were. If, however, your context for love is a continuum of successive eternal instants, you can tap into the infinite each moment and expand your life urge without limits. The key is in the way you think. As your mind turns, so goes your life.

Whenever you worry about the future, whether it's the future of your job, relationship, or body, it is always the fear of death you are unconsciously feeling. And when you obsess on the future, time flies, and your fears loom larger. When you focus on the eternal, life-nurturing qualities of life, you bathe in a sea of immortality. You might even be amazed by the new dimensions of love you get to experience.

It is not necessarily true that all good things come to an end. That's just one thought of many on the subject.

AFFIRMATIONS

1. *My life urge is stronger than my death urge.*

2. *Since my life urge is so strong, I can survive my unconscious death urge.*

3. *My partner and I can survive our collective death urge.*

4. *I never have to leave to survive.*

5. *I choose life even in the middle of thoughts of death.*

6. *My love rejuvenates me.*

7. *Surrendering to my partner's love replenishes my life urge.*

8. *I am never separate from life.*

9. *I forgive my parents for their death urge.*

10. *I can stay alive and not lose my parents' love.*

11. *I don't have to join my ancestors to be connected to my roots.*

12. *My roots nurture my life urge.*

13. *My relationship is grounded in life.*

14. *I no longer push love away when my death urge is up.*

15. *The more love I let in, the faster I release my death urge.*

16. *My desire to be intimate is greater than my addiction to separation.*

17. *My life is potentially unlimited.*

18. *My life is unlimited.*

19. *I see all things as possible.*

20. *I am safe and immortal in the present moment.*

—15—

Silence Is Golden

George and Martha found a new level of intimacy together. Going through so much death stuff made life more sacred for them. And releasing so much fear opened them to a sensitivity they had never felt before.

While George was in the hospital, Martha would sit at his bedside and pray in silence, or read to him from the Psalms or Yogananda's Meditations. George's jaw was badly broken and he couldn't talk for six weeks. When he came home, the habit of silence stayed with them, and they hardly ever broke it. They were like dancers. Their bodies did all the talking.

At first Martha judged their quiet. She knew that lack of communication was one of the ten danger signs in any relationship. But then she realized that there was no lack of communication between them. In fact she had never felt so connected to another human being. It seemed like their minds spilled over into one another, like two full cups overflowing.

She would think of a walk on the beach, and he would get up to go. He would think of a drive to the desert, and she'd be filling their canteen. They began to meditate together, not from a conscious choice to impose a spiritual discipline on their lives. It just happened. One night they found themselves sitting on the living room floor staring at a candle for three hours. The flame seemed to kindle and nourish a need they had, so they continued flame-watching without ever discussing it.

Martha turned one of their spare bedrooms into a little spiritual retreat. She hung pictures of spiritual places all over the walls—the Taj

Mahal, the Church of the Holy Sepulchre, Lourdes, Notre Dame, St. Patrick's. The only piece of furniture in the room was a small altar with three candles on it and a little bronze statue David had brought back from his recent trip to India. A statue of Shiva.

Alex Kaplan thought they were getting a little weird, but he kept his mouth shut. He could see there was a new light between George and Martha, and he figured that where there's light there's a spark—and that was what mattered the most.

They began taking yoga classes together, at first to rehabilitate George's back, but later because it supported this new connection and seemed to stretch their minds yet further. A profound peace settled over them. And a subtle passion.

Their lovemaking moved from the physical and romantic to the mystical and metaphysical. Again, they never consciously sat down and said, hey why don't we try this. It just sort of happened, naturally. They'd spend hours in a sweet, passionate embrace, every touch generating new electricity between them. They discovered places in their bodies they never even knew had feeling. Suddenly, there was new life where there had been numbness, new openness where fear had once shut things down. At times the pleasure between them was so exquisite that one or both of them would emit a long sweet wail, almost like an Om, and the sound would carry them to rapture and bliss.

They began to see things they couldn't talk about even if they had been talking: colors, auras, energy fields, and the wonderful Being that came to them. They knew she was a gift, this radiant light-being that hovered over them throughout George's recovery.

Martha had noticed her first. One morning when they were meditating by the altar, she felt a strong presence enter the room. She turned her head and George followed her gaze. And there behind them, by the picture of Lourdes, she hovered, a soft amber glow at first, but then—there could be no mistaking it—an angel, a childlike cherub with a golden halo, smiling and reaching out to them, offering her blessing.

They knew she was their guardian angel, and they felt her light whenever she was near them.

They began to listen to holy music together, and to chant some simple Sanskrit songs they learned from their yoga teacher. George learned to play the flute and Martha the piano. They spent days just making up music together.

The simpler their lives became, the more joy they felt between them.

Martha was dressing differently now. Pastels replaced the blacks and the blues, and her paintings were different, too, full of childlike shapes, colors, and designs. She thought of this as her "period of innocence."

George eventually went back to work. He took the part of a deaf soldier in the Civil War. And he agreed to be a regular on a new TV series about a karate master and his rebel son. Neither of the projects started filming until the summer. And it was only March.

So the long hours of sweet nothing continued. One night they were meditating and George turned to look at Martha. He just meditated on her beauty, which had become bigger than life to him. She had always been a knockout, but now all her chakras seemed to be exploding in harmonic magnificence. God, he thought, where is she taking me?

He only knew he loved her more than words could say.

WAY #15: SILENCE IS GOLDEN

So often words get in the way. We usually think that communication is 90% verbal and 10% non-verbal. The truth is just the opposite.

So much of what we actually say to each other is either idle chatter, inappropriate attack or self-defense—our minds' noise, clutter and internal conflict projected outwards. What we call communication might more aptly be termed mental regurgitation.

The art of listening is the better part of communication. Not just listening to your partner without defense, hearing what he or she really has to say, which is, of course, extremely important. But even more important is listening to yourself, your voice within, your intuition. Two people, each of whom has access to his or her inner voice, can hear each other clearly, so clearly that they often have little to say to each other.

Telepathy springs from this well of inner communion. A sacred silence replaces frustrated conversation. Harmony replaces conflict. When both partners sink into this deep silence, they discover a new language.

We all need to calm down, relax, feel the quiet truth, which in the middle of silence is clear as a bell. We all need to let go of urgency, anxiety, and worry. Silence is a good place to start.

Simple spiritual practices can change your whole universe overnight.

However, these practices work best when they evolve naturally rather than as a technique you impose on your life for specific purposes. They can help you get your busy mind out of the way. They can strengthen your heart energy. They can awaken you to new dimensions of your own being.

We are all like a mountain stream rushing over a rock. The stream is busy, constantly changing, coming and going, never the same. The rock is still and unchanging, nowhere to go, just to be.

The stream is our busy little minds. The rock is our quiet center.

Build the temple on the rock.

AFFIRMATIONS

1. *My spirituality enhances my relationships.*

2. *The more I am connected to God, the more connected I am to my partner.*

3. *It's safe to be silent.*

4. *I love the sound of silence.*

5. *All my relationships are sacred.*

6. *My partner and I share a holy purpose together.*

7. *God takes care of my loving relationship.*

8. *It's safe to listen to my own inner voice.*

9. *I can hear my intuition clearly.*

10. *My connection to spirit nurtures my relationship.*

11. *My spiritual and physical universes support one another.*

12. *It's fun to be spiritual.*

13. *My spirituality leads me into the world.*

14. *I can be peaceful and passionate.*

15. *I can be both detached and involved.*

16. *When I listen to my inner voice, I hear my partner better.*

17. *My peace needs no defense.*

18. *I can see the divinity in everyone.*

19. *I hear my partner beyond his/her words.*

20. *I listen for the truth, not idle chatter.*

—16—

It Takes All Kinds

They lived like hermits for two months, hibernating in the cave of silence they had discovered. Alex Kaplan was missing them as were Martha's mom and sisters. George's mother and father were worried and wanted him to visit New York. David Levy insisted that they all get together.

So they decided to come out of their shell. They realized that it was one thing to be holy in isolation but another thing entirely to share that holiness in the world. What they most wanted now was balance in their lives.

They threw a party, a counter-inauguration party. It was January 22, 1969. Nixon was being sworn in. David asked George, "Why celebrate?"

"Because," he replied, "the impossible has happened; therefore, anything is possible." David instantly realized that his friend had been through a major transformation.

Sally and her girlfriend Beth were smooching in public. Martha's mom walked around saying, "What next, what next?" George told Martha he was glad Sally was so happy, and she smiled and kissed him.

Karen, the younger sister, was having a rough time. She was drinking too much and saying things like, "Nixon's not so bad. I think he's kind of sexy." David Levy took her hand and led her out to the beach where they walked for some time. He asked her how she was doing.

"Me? I'm fine. I'm the normal one, remember?"

"Yeah, but what's normal?"

"Oh come on, David, you know what I'm talking about."

Meanwhile, Martha was showing her father their altar. Alex Kaplan considered himself broad-minded. He had not voted for Nixon. But his limits were being stretched to the max.

"What's this?" he asked, lifting the little statue.

"That's Shiva. David brought it from India."

"And who is Shiva?"

"Shiva is an androgynous goddess—the giver and taker of life, the master player."

"Sounds like she should be president."

"I'd vote for her."

Alex looked around at all the holy places on the walls.

"Are you still Jewish, Martha?"

"Yes, Dad. I am what I am."

"Then why?" he motioned with a sweeping gesture of his cigar.

"It just feels right, Dad. I don't expect you or Mom to understand."

"Try me, baby."

"Well, after the accident, things changed. We needed to be different, you know. We needed a new direction."

"Maybe you should move to Santa Barbara. It's very quiet, I hear."

"Not that kind of direction, Dad. Inner direction."

"Inner direction?"

"Yes. Remember, you used to quote Shakespeare all the time—'To thine own self be true, and it must follow, as the night the day, thou canst not then be false to any man'?"

"Polonius, no?"

"Yes, Dad. Well, it was great advice but I never knew who I was."

"You should have asked. I would have told you."

"Told me what?"

"You're the greatest girl on earth!"

Martha gave him a big hug.

George was talking to Sarah, Martha's mom, who couldn't take her eyes off Sally and Beth, still caressing each other. Sally was hugging Beth from behind as she cooked enchiladas, her hands cupped over Beth's substantial breasts.

"How are you feeling, Sarah?"

"Me? Oh great, George. Think of it this way. I lost one breast, but I gained two." George laughed.

"It's rough watching the girls, huh?"

"Oh no, it's not rough. The chemotherapy, that's rough. I lose my hair. This, all I lose is my mind."

George toasted Sarah and they sipped Perrier. Sarah needed something stronger so George got her a scotch and soda. They sat down to watch Nixon's speech. After a few minutes, Sarah was weeping.

"I miss Bobby Kennedy so much."

"Me, too."

"He was like the son I never had. Nixon. I look at him and I feel sorry for his mother."

"I feel sorry for the world."

"Oh George, what's the world coming to?"

"Maybe Karen's right. Maybe he'll surprise us."

"I'm tired of surprises."

"It takes all kinds, I guess."

David was telling Karen about two gay actors he represented who dressed up as women and pretended to be lesbians. She was laughing at his description.

"And the funny thing is, when they're girls, they make all these snide comments about gay men."

"The world is nuts, David. Absolutely cashew!"

"It takes all kinds, Karen. All kinds."

Alex Kaplan walked his daughter onto the terrace. He had one arm around her and the other held the Havana in his mouth. They watched the sun go down. The L.A. smog added special effects to the natural color show.

"It takes all kinds, Martha. Jews, Arabs, Catholics, Protestants, hippies, dykes and shivas—all kinds." Martha laughed.

"I guess," continued Alex, pointing to the sun with his cigar, "the same sun shines on all of us."

Way #16: It Takes All Kinds

The mind is tempted to judge all differences. To the mind, diversity is a threat and sameness is security. That's how boring our minds get.

It's time to start celebrating our differences. If the planet is going to make it, let alone our relationships, we need to stop trying to mold others into our own image. It's far healthier to let go of our image.

The mind is addicted to familiarity. It wants everything to be like it was in the good old days, even if they really weren't half as good as they seem in retrospect. Your heart wants to open things up, experience new love and energy, stretch. Follow your heart, not your mind.

Have the courage to be different. Have the strength to be innocent. If you're gay, be gay. If you're a mystic, be a mystic. If you're in love with the President, speak up. And give others the space to be different, too. Let go of your judgments of others, and you will free yourself to come out of the closet. Let's face it, we often judge people the most when they have the courage we are sorely lacking.

God created us in His own image, so His image must be changing all the time—male, female, black, white, red, yellow, Catholic, Jew. When we're threatened by such overwhelming differences, we create holy wars. Someone once said that all wars were essentially holy wars, even the battle between the sexes. Perhaps the deeper truth is, no war is holy. Life is sacred. How could the taking of lives be holy no matter what the justification?

Variety is the spice of life. Don't try to cook Indian food with French seasoning. Life is not bland and uniform by nature. It's unnatural to want to make it all the same. Yet there is a common thread, a Oneness, a unifying energy behind all apparent diversity. The trick is to find the balance.

No two relationships are the same. That's why it never works to compare your relationship to someone else's.

It takes all kinds.

AFFIRMATIONS

1. *It's safe to be different.*
2. *It's safe to let my differences show.*
3. *My difference makes a difference.*
4. *I allow other people their differences.*
5. *I celebrate differences.*
6. *I celebrate diversity.*
7. *I forgive myself for judging others when they are different.*
8. *I forgive myself for judging myself.*
9. *I forgive others for judging me.*
10. *There is no difference worth fighting over.*
11. *I'm one of a kind.*
12. *Everyone is one of a kind.*
13. *I love my partner's differences.*
14. *Whenever I differ, I stretch.*
15. *Whenever I embrace differences, I grow.*
16. *Even in the best of families there are differences.*
17. *I don't have to be like my parents to win their love.*
18. *I have the courage to be myself.*
19. *I respect others for their courage in being themselves.*
20. *It takes all kinds to make a perfect planet.*

—17—

Get Back to Where You Once Came From

George and Martha wrote me occasionally, so I could keep up with the progress of their "case," as they liked to call it. I often wrote them back with suggestions and new ideas that had come to me. In one letter they complained about there being no role models for the relationship they wanted. They wondered why I didn't share more about my own relationship. I wrote back saying that I thought role models were an obsolete concept, that if you tried to imitate someone else's relationship, you just ended up not being yourself. It would be like two doves copying two dolphins. Carry on, I encouraged them.

George was soon to start shooting his karate series in Hawaii, where he hadn't been since he was a child. He and Martha decided to take a one-month's vacation before going to work, so they flew to Kauai in early May. Their relationship was in its third year, and they had been through many changes. But the biggest changes were still to come.

They stayed at a villa on a spectacular cliff overlooking a pure, white-sand beach. A cook came with the villa and his name was Jimmy Ho. Jimmy was a forty-five-year-old native Hawaiian, with bright brown eyes and a winning smile.

"Aloha," he greeted them. "Welcome to Kauai."

"Aloha," George and Martha replied.

After a while Jimmy started cooking, and George and Martha unpacked and then meditated for twenty minutes. Jimmy watched them out of the corner of his eye while humming an island tune.

They sat down to the fabulous feast Jimmy had prepared—fresh fruit and salad, and a local fish neither of them recognized. They invited him to join them for dinner, and he thanked them but said he must go. But before he went he wished to make a prayer for them, which delighted them. Jimmy sat down opposite Martha, dropped his head, and placed his hands together.

"Oh, Heavenly Father, we thank you for this island of Kauai. If we have ever caused any harm here, now or in any previous incarnation, we ask the island to forgive us our trespasses. Oh, Heavenly Father, we thank you for this wonderful food, and if we have ever caused any harm, now or in any previous incarnation, we ask this fish, this fruit, these salad greens and every grain of salt and pepper to forgive us our trespasses. Amen."

George and Martha looked at each other and shrugged their shoulders simultaneously as Jimmy concluded his blessing.

"Thank you, oh Heavenly Father." He took a slow deep breath and, lifting his head, exhaled.

"Thank you," he said to them. "My kahuna taught me that."

"It's very interesting," Martha said.

"You would like to meet her?"

"Well, yes."

"I ask her to come tomorrow."

"Thank you, Jimmy," George said as Jimmy bowed and left.

A kahuna is a Hawaiian priest or priestess, in possession of ancient secrets, rites, and practices. George and Martha had both heard wonderful stories and were eager to meet a real-life kahuna. The next day came and went. After dinner Martha asked Jimmy when the kahuna was coming.

"Tomorrow."

Tomorrow passed and still no kahuna. Three days later and still nothing. Jimmy told them that kahunas move in their own time and they should be patient and prepare. Finally, on their fifth day in Kauai, Jimmy brought the kahuna, who turned out to be well worth the wait. Her name was Hana, and she was much younger than they expected, although the more they looked at her the more impossible it was to determine her age. Hana had long black hair down to her waist, a voluptuous body, and big black eyes with beaming white light exploding from them. Her power was obvious and her radiant presence seemed to spread across the entire room.

They all sat down, and Hana recited a prayer she called the "Peace of I." Then she performed a ceremony called "Ho'Opono Pono" which she said would cleanse their pasts. Afterwards, they all meditated. Neither George nor Martha had ever meditated so deeply. Hana's presence seemed to take them places they never knew existed, and they experienced two past lives together, which, when they shared later, matched up. In one, George was a cat burglar in eighteenth-century France and Martha a famous sleuth, chasing him across rooftops. In the other, Martha was a rich Roman male and George one of his concubines who longed for freedom and tried several times to escape. Each time he, or she, was captured, punished, and finally died from her wounds at age 28.

"Jesus!" George exclaimed, "No wonder I'm always running away from you. You really are out to get me." Martha laughed. George realized he was now 28 years old, and there might be some correlation there. In truth, they thought it was all a bit far out, but they were intrigued beyond their skepticism. Hana told them a few other things. She said she saw that they had been to Kauai before, in ancient times. They were astronauts from outer space, and they invaded Kauai, destroying villages and raping the land.

"Heavy karma," Jimmy commented.

"I ask the Unihipili to forgive these two, who come now in love and peace." (The Unihipili, Jimmy later explained, is the God within.) Martha was so moved she cried. Hana nodded her head. She suggested they do karma yoga to clean the slate. So they decided they would cook for Jimmy for a month instead of the other way around. Jimmy loved this idea and asked if he could bring some friends once in a while.

"One more thing," said Hana. "Have you ever been to Bermuda?"

"No."

"You must be very careful when you go there. You must pray for forgiveness even before you go." She refused to tell them why.

When Hana and Jimmy left, George and Martha felt much lighter, as though an old heavy burden had indeed been lifted from their hearts.

WAY #17: GET BACK TO WHERE YOU ONCE CAME FROM

You might find the entire concept of past lives a little hard to swallow. Certainly, it would be difficult to prove scientifically. But this is not a textbook so much as a guidebook. And allowing your mind to be guided to places you do not normally visit can only increase your understanding of yourself, your relationships, and the mysterious forces at work in your life. And you don't have to swallow the whole concept in order to taste the idea.

When you do a past life regression, whether you are actually remembering a historical truth stored in your unconsciousness or are simply creating a past from your subconscious desires is of secondary importance. Even if you are making it up, it is no accident that you make up what you make up. So think of a past life as a metaphor to shed more light on your current one. And if it feels very real to you, think of it as a very real metaphor. Do not use a past life as an excuse for avoiding this one. Always see the past, be it your childhood, birth, or a previous existence, as a means of being more here and now.

If you discover a past life in which you and your partner were in conflict, forgive each other and let that life go. If there was a major incompletion or lack of resolution on some issue that is currently operative, look for the solution now.

Karma is the idea that we all have past debts we are required to pay back, and that in completing our karmic debts we attain more wholeness, peace, and balance in our lives. Karma is simply the concept of cause and effect from the spiritual point of view.

It is possible to complete all karmic debts now and to climb off the great wheel of unknown fortune that keeps us spinning in circles.

Affirmations

1. I am willing to pay back all my karmic debts.

2. I am willing to complete all karma now.

3. I never have to suffer in order to complete karma.

4. I am innocent even though I have karma.

5. Since karma means cause and effect, the more I discover the cause of my karma, the freer I am of the effects.

6. I forgive myself for all my past life mistakes.

7. I forgive others for all the pain they caused me.

8. I am willing to do whatever karma yoga is appropriate.

9. I complete my debts joyfully.

10. No matter who I was in a past life, I am always me.

11. There is no escape from myself.

12. I am free to be myself.

13. I look to the past to free myself more, not to find excuses for failure.

14. All my past lives are with me now.

15. I have access to Infinite Intelligence and therefore all information about my spiritual history.

16. My desire to see the whole truth is greater than my fear and skepticism.

17. I am never threatened by the past.

18. It's safe to see a past life.

19. I am grateful for all my lives.

20. My relationship is enriched by past life information.

—18—

Beware of High Woo

George and Martha sat with Hana on two other occasions during the following week, and both times they were humbled by her peace, wisdom, joy, and sweetness. On one occasion George offered her $100 but she would accept no money. "We exchange from the heart, not from the wallet," she said.

They had a private beach below the cliff all to themselves. There they would sunbathe in the nude, snorkel, and commune with the spirits of Kauai in silence. George played his flute. Martha painted watercolors of all kinds of fish. They made long, lasting love whenever the urge came. They seemed to be guided by an ancient pulsating rhythm throughout each day. Time stopped completely, and the gates of eternity swung wide open. Their whole life, past, present, and future, seemed to be with them all at once. They were utterly defenseless. And safe.

One day a helicopter appeared out of nowhere and landed. Two huge Hawaiian men emerged, dressed in blue jeans and red flowery rayon shirts. They appeared to be twins.

"Aloha," one waved, and they both approached as George and Martha put on their cut-off jeans. They were very large men, like sumo wrestlers.

"Aloha," George greeted them. "Can we help you?" It was an absurd question. Obviously, these two bruisers had not invaded their beach to ask directions. They all sat down, and the one who was talking introduced them.

"We are the Gemini twins." When he saw that neither George nor

Martha recognized the name, he proceeded, "We have been on national television."

"Oh?" said Martha.

"We are gurus."

George felt like laughing but didn't. He also felt something ominous about these two.

"My brother is mute. He speaks only in thoughts. He is a clear channel. I translate his thoughts. We have a strong psychic connection."

"I see." Martha was open to anything at this point.

"In a way he is the ventriloquist and I am the dummy. Only he is the dummy. Ha, ha, ha!" George laughed with him.

"We have a commune up in the mountains. In the valley of a thousand rainbows. Have you been there?"

"No," said Martha, curious.

"You want to come with us?"

"Maybe tomorrow," said George.

"You should come see it. It is very beautiful. We have one hundred followers who live there. We farm and sing and pray together. And we dig a big tunnel into the crater."

"Why?" asked Martha.

"We are looking for a huge heartstone left by the ancient astronauts."

"I see."

"You should come see." George didn't like the pressure he was feeling. "It is so beautiful. Just to be there will empty your minds forever."

"I bet," said George.

"What happens when you find the heartstone?" asked Martha.

"It is alive, you know. It beats like a real heart. But after 10,000 years it is very weak. Only my brother can hear it and only if it is very quiet and he puts his ear to the earth at the right spot."

"Fascinating," Martha commented.

"When we find it, the ancient astronauts will return and take us to their planet. Hopefully before the boys in Washington and Moscow blow us off this one. Ha, ha, ha!"

George was open to the idea of UFOs, even ancient astronauts, but this was too far out even for his stretched mind. Martha, however, was totally defenseless. She accepted all input without judgement. She would have believed anything.

"You should come with us now. We have come to get you."

"But you don't even know us."

"Jimmy Ho is a friend of ours. He told us what Hana said about you. My brother thought about it for a long time. He says you should not leave this island without seeing the work we do. My brother thinks it may have been you who buried the heartstone so many years ago. If so, you might remember where it is and help us. Please come."

"Oh, let's go, George."

"But Martha . . ."

"It's another adventure."

"But Martha . . ."

"Don't be a wimp, George."

"We will return you in one hour." So the four of them flew off in the helicopter.

What they saw flying over the interior of Kauai was breathtaking. Volcanoes and craters and hundreds of huge waterfalls and rainbows and fertile valleys. They landed in one such valley in the middle of it all.

There were dozens of tents pitched around a big log cabin. When they emerged from the helicopter, Gemini showed them the dig where about thirty-five young people, most of whom appeared to be straight off their surfboards, were busy working. They looked totally mindless and they chanted OM over and over again. George got the creeps. Martha seemed spaced out.

George noticed there were several guards, carrying shotguns, stationed at various strategic points. When he inquired, Gemini told him, "It is a necessary precaution. The FBI, you know." George didn't know, but he could guess. When he saw the silent twin handing Martha a fat joint, he was already planning a getaway. Gemini lit a second joint and passed it to George.

"You've heard of Maui Wowie? This here is Kauai Highee—it's a complete knockout."

"I bet," said George, sizing up the whole scene.

"You should stay here with us. It is home, you know. So much love. Yes, we are one big happy family. Ha, ha, ha!"

Cult, George was thinking. Martha wasn't thinking anything. She was stoned out of her mind.

"I'll tell you what," said Gemini. "If you give me, say, $25,000, you can stay here until we find the heartstone. Then you can go to the other planet with us, when the ancient astronauts come, if the boys in Washington and Moscow don't push the button first. Ha, ha, ha!"

Gemini's laugh was enough to kill any serious sense of humor. George was trying to play it cool and, quite frankly, the dope was making it extremely challenging to concentrate on any thought. He looked over at Martha and realized that she was his silent partner just like Gemini's twin.

"It is paradise here. Just $35,000."

"$35,000?" George responded, not commenting on the sudden inflation in the cult's economy. "Sounds reasonable enough. Hmm. Let me see. How's about you fly us back to our little villa. Then we can make all the necessary phone calls, arrangements, you know, get the money . . . yeah, you fly us back, we get the money, then you can pick us up, say tomorrow late afternoon?"

Gemini took a long drag on the joint.

"Sounds good to me," his voice sounded like helium as he slowly exhaled the marijuana. "You know, I saw you in a movie once. Something about a temple in Mexico."

"You saw that?" George was genuinely astonished.

"Yes. I used to live in Venice. A lot of these kids are from L.A., you know."

"They look like Hollywood extras."

"Their parents would shit bricks if they could see them now. Ha, ha, ha!"

Gemini I and II flew George and Martha back to the villa. George waved goodbye as they flew off in the helicopter, then ran into the villa, picked up the phone and made plans to fly to L.A. the next day.

Martha asked why.

"Baby," he said, holding her in his arms, "Let's not lose it entirely."

"What do you mean, honey?"

"Open your eyes, sweetheart. We are definitely in over our heads."

Way #18: Beware of High Woo

To be spiritual is not to be stupid. Spiritual wisdom is the result of filtering mind-expanding experiences through common sense. The purpose of spiritual growth is personal well-being, as well as opening one's heart to global compassion, and there are many gifted teachers, healers, psychics, and sensitives who can give you a "power assist" on your path towards self-realization.

There are also, unfortunately, an abundance of false prophets along the way.

When you open yourself to the spiritual world, you are vulnerable to all sorts of influences. You are releasing the judgmental part of your mind in order to experience other dimensions. This renders you vulnerable to many people who might take advantage of your highly impressionable state of being. It is important that you practice spiritual discrimination even while surrendering and letting go of control. This can be a delicate balance.

To be spiritual is not to be naive. Remember, your purpose is to claim your own power, intuition, inner voice, and to discover your holy purpose in being alive. Learning to discern a false prophet from a true guide, a healthy spiritual family from a cult, is part of the process.

A false prophet is one who leads you away from yourself in the name of God. He (or she) therefore reinforces the thought of separation, telling you that if you devote yourself to a separate source of truth, namely himself, you will see the light and be free. He tells you that there is a spiritual hierarchy, that he is higher on the ladder than you, and that you must submit your will to his in order to climb higher. This is nonsense.

The truth is, spirituality is equality. We are all spiritually equal if diverse; we are a multiple guru system in which we are all teaching each other important lessons daily. Spiritual arrogance is just as off the track as any kind of arrogance. Spirituality without humility is the ego masquerading as an all-powerful God.

It is important that you learn to recognize the difference between "High Woo," i.e., false spirituality, and the real thing. The ego is a slippery devil and can pose as all things high and holy. It can speak of miracles, love, and healing. It can chant, trance, and meditate. The ego is a three-ring circus with all sorts of acts, clowns, and daredevils. As such, it can be quite entertaining. But one thing the ego is not is Spirit. On the contrary, the ego's very existence lies in the belief that we are separate from Spirit.

The ego is a seductive fool who will woo you away from yourself until you wake up and recognize the grand deception. When you are blinded by your own ego, you will tend to see the light in someone else's.

When you walk in the light of God, someone else's ego is just a shadow along the path.

A friend of mine uses the term High Woo to describe all the spiritual flakes who try to woo us with false promises of greater enlightenment. Beware of spiritual flakes. High Woo is seduction masquerading as spirituality.

AFFIRMATIONS

1. *I am the source of my own spirituality.*

2. *I never have to give my power away in order to grow.*

3. *I never leave myself in order to find myself.*

4. *I can recognize the difference between a guide on the path and an unnecessary detour.*

5. *I trust my intuition more than anyone's authority.*

6. *I know a cult when I see one.*

7. *I know a spiritual family when I see one.*

8. *I reject all psychics who flatter my ego.*

9. *I know it is love, not power, that heals.*

10. *My spirituality is not a function of fad but of truth.*

11. *I have a personal relationship with God I can trust.*

12. *My spirituality supports harmony in all my relationships.*

13. *I can be open and discriminating at the same time.*

14. *I have a sense of spiritual wisdom.*

15. *My spirituality is practical, not escapist.*

16. *I surrender to God and myself and nobody else.*

17. *Since I'm grateful for my past, I never have to reject it in the name of spirituality.*

18. *I know a flake when I meet one.*

19. *I am never seduced by leaders.*

20. *When I trust myself, I know what's true and what's false.*

—19—

Be Open to Divine Intervention

The next morning Martha realized just how far over her head she had sunk. When she woke up, she was no longer stoned, and she put together the pieces of the Gemini twins and the valley of a thousand rainbows.

"Jesus Christ!" she said to herself. "Jesus Christ!!" It was 7:00 AM George was still sleeping. She remembered he had booked them out on a noon flight, bless his discriminating heart!

She got out of bed and walked onto the terrace. The sun was just rising, and she felt compelled to feel the sea one more time. She took her face mask, snorkel, and flippers and climbed down the cliff to the deserted beach. She removed her purple nightgown and looked out at the ocean. The sound of the waves beating against the rocks was the only sound. There was a small cave she walked into and then she sat on a flat rock, meditating. She spoke out loud, "Forgive us our trespasses, you very sweet island, and forgive me any pain I have caused George in this or any past lifetime."

She breathed deeply for several minutes, then said aloud, "He is a good man. I love him with all my soul. I pray he never leaves me again." She meditated in silence for another ten minutes, then put on her gear and swam out to sea.

The Pacific Ocean is really misnamed. The Atlantic is far more pacific than the Pacific, and in Hawaii the misleading Mother can be a seductive, deceptive bitch. Swimming off the Kauaian shores, Martha was on her own, and she was clearly in over her head, though she didn't realize it for another fifteen minutes. She was a strong swimmer, too, and she was thoroughly absorbed by the swarms of psychedelic fish she saw through her mask. And there were two dolphins accompanying her, escorting her like sea-angels, as the subtle current pulled her gently but steadily away from George.

George felt the pull. It woke him up with a jolt. His first thought was, "Gemini." Then he reached out for Martha who was not there. He jumped out of bed and looked all over for her, but she was nowhere in sight. Gemini fuckers, he muttered to himself, and thought of dialing the police emergency number. But something pulled at him and he went out to the terrace and watched the sea kick up. There was a strong wind blowing east to west. It was 9:00 AM.

Martha was in trouble, but she refused to admit it. Rather than struggle to swim back, she surrendered to the tide and the current and drifted further out. The two dolphins continued to swim with her, and a part of her mind said her safety was in their hands. Or flippers.

George noticed Martha's purple nightgown on the white sand, and he looked out across the sea for her, but she was still nowhere to be seen. He was frightened. And his fear of losing her pumped him up. He had to spring into action. So he called the police.

Martha was swallowing too much water. She struggled now to swim back to shore, but she wasn't making any progress. It seemed like the ocean could push her with more power than she could push it. Her breath was short and her memory long. She was thinking about her very first swimming lesson, when her dad taught her to kick while holding his hands in the Beverly Hills pool. God, how she wished she were there now. Holding Dad's hands. Oh George, where are you? I need you!

He couldn't bear waiting, so he went back outside. He thought he heard a voice calling, so he climbed down the cliff to the white sand beach. It was quiet except for the waves crashing against the cliff.

Martha was splashing a lot, flailing her arms about 100 yards out. She could see George on the sand but didn't have the energy to shout. Suddenly, the dolphins darted off towards shore, squealing, crying, calling out for George's attention.

George didn't notice anything unusual at first. He saw the dolphins and almost smiled. There were always dolphins in the morning. Martha loved to swim with them. They were so peaceful. Then he realized, not these two!

Martha's whole life flashed by in an instant, so she knew the end was near. She saw her birth in living color, and, bad as it was, she would have traded her death for her birth a thousand times. She saw scenes from her infancy, childhood, adolescence. Fights with her sisters. Her first sexual experience. (She almost died on that one.) Philip. George. She saw everything, and when the movie was over, she thought she must be dead.

George was swimming like Mark Spitz. The dolphins guided him. He knew she was there, somewhere. God, the sea was rough. Martha!

She prayed for a miracle, salvation, or instant reincarnation. She couldn't stand the uncertainty. She hated the twilight zone. Then she thought she heard a child, a little boy's voice calling, "Mommy, Mommy, don't drown." She remembered thinking, that's absurd, I don't have a son. And she thought she remembered seeing, right near the end, before everything went black, the amber glow of their guardian angel, smiling, signalling something.

George finally saw her, her head bobbing in and out of the water, her arms flailing. He swam over to her and lifted her up. He was exhausted and could barely hold himself above water, let alone Martha. He noticed the dolphins and had an idea. Using all his strength, he pulled her body on top of one of the dolphins, then grabbed the other one himself. The dolphins cooperated beautifully, swimming towards the shore with their friends on their backs. They were going to make it, George realized; thank God, they were going to make it.

They both lay on the sand, breathing heavily.

"George?"

"Martha?"

"I thought I was dead."

"Close but no cigar."

"My whole life flashed by."

"I bet."

"I'm glad I'm alive. God, am I glad."

"Me too, sweetie, me too."

WAY #19: BE OPEN TO DIVINE INTERVENTION

Be open to miracles. God knows, we all need them once in a while.

The ancient Greek dramatists often had surprise endings for their plays, sudden twists at the very end. The hero, for instance, would be about to die, and suddenly, the deus ex machina would appear—a huge crane towering above the stage would lower a god who would save the day and assure a happy ending.

Without such divine intervention from time to time, no relationship could survive. Sometimes it's as simple as being in the middle of an argument and looking up to see a rainbow. Suddenly, all that "fight energy" evaporates. Or you're in the middle of a screaming match and suddenly a child laughs, and then you are laughing for no reason at all. Where does the rainbow come from? Or the child's laughter? Deus ex machina. *Divine intervention.*

Always look for a sign from God. A sign to guide you to the next step. A sign of right action. A sign of peace. A love sign. God is a prolific sign-maker.

Sometimes God intervenes in mysterious ways. You're walking out on your lover and you trip over your own two feet, sprain your ankle, and have to lie down for three days. You're getting in your car to drive off into the sunset, never to see her again, and the car won't start. And the airport is fogged in. And the taxis are on strike. And the bus drivers have joined in in sympathy. God can make some pretty funny signs when He's in the mood.

And sometimes He sends you a dolphin to save you from drowning.

AFFIRMATIONS

1. *I am always open to miracles.*

2. *I recognize a miracle when I see one.*

3. *There is an abundance of daily miracles in my life.*

4. *I expect miracles.*

5. *God is there whenever I call.*

6. *God sends me a sign whenever I ask.*

7. *I know how to interpret God's signs.*

8. *God has a great sense of timing.*

9. *God doesn't have to part the Red Sea for me to notice His presence.*

10. *God's presence is everywhere.*

11. *God is with me; I am never alone.*

12. *Even in my darkest hour, God sheds light.*

13. *God never leaves me.*

14. *I forgive myself for trying to keep God out.*

15. *Things can change in an instant.*

16. *Problems can disappear overnight.*

17. *All miracles are equally simple in God's mind.*

18. *I can now see miracles in the obvious.*

19. *I'm always at the right time and place to witness a miracle.*

20. *God sends me one message and the message is love.*

—20—

All Roads Lead to Home

It was Thanksgiving, 1969. They had lived together for three years. Martha was withdrawing in little ways. She was psychically keeping George at a distance. Really, there are 10,000 ways to leave your lover without even setting your foot out the door. Martha was mastering all the little ways. George, on the other hand, was plain old restless and beginning to look at other women. Nothing subtle about George.

The funny thing was there was no apparent cause to this new turn of events. The last six months had been a period of tremendous ease and pleasure between them. The Hawaiian adventure had deepened their bond, George's career was soaring, and Martha was painting up a storm. Their lovemaking was sweet and satisfying. They were meditating, chanting, walking on the beach arm-in-arm. Then, two weeks before Thanksgiving, this new separation spread its wings.

Martha's mom cooked a huge turkey, and the whole gang came over. David Levy, too. David was looking fit and trim; he had been working out. Martha, noticing the results, was drawn to him in a new way. George felt the energy between them but said nothing. Karen was flirting with him as usual, and Sally and Beth were as affectionate as ever. It was a family gathering.

It was unusually hot for November. Alex Kaplan was in great spirits and had been since the Mets won the World Series a month before. He had won $25,000 on that one. Alex loved a good underdog. After dinner, he took George out by the pool, lit his Havana, and they walked together like father and son.

"Did you ever want to leave, Alex?"

"Leave? Leave all this?" he circled his world with the smoke from his cigar. "You gotta be nuts."

"Never?"

"Well, I mean, of course I've had the thought. Everyone does. I mean, it comes up. All the pressure. It gets to you. I used to have fantasies about disappearing. You know, the ones where you change your name, move to nowhere in Texas and start all over again. I'd never do it, mind you. But it's a nice fantasy."

"Why wouldn't you do it?"

"Well, three reasons. One, I just wouldn't. Too many responsibilities. Too many people to take care of. Secondly, I love what I do too much. I'd be crazy to blow it. I've worked hard to get this far. And third, even if I left, I figure I'd end up back here. I mean, all I know is this, so if I didn't have it, I'd make it up again. Then what would I do? Leave again? And again?"

"It's a vicious cycle, I guess."

"You thinking of splitting, George?"

"It's come up. No reason really."

"Let me tell you a story, son." Alex put his arm around George and steered him towards the canyon. "When I was a kid growing up in Brooklyn, I used to dream about running away every night. I always knew I'd end up in California. It seemed like a big mistake that I was born in Brooklyn. Like I had landed by spaceship, 3000 miles off course. You know what I'm saying?"

"Yes."

"I always had a terrible sense of direction."

"Me, too. Martha's the navigator."

"She's got that internal compass and a mind map of the universe. Some kid."

"Some of us get lost, some do the finding."

"Exactly. Anyway, there I am, lost in Brooklyn, hating everything, even the Dodgers. I'm six years old and planning my escape. So one night, when my parents are asleep, I pack a little knapsack and sneak out. I go out on the street and start walking. I walk and I walk and I walk and I walk. I mean, I've always been a walker, but that night I outdid myself."

"Where did you go?"

"Nowhere. I just walked. When I was tired, I got a cab. I had $10 saved, so I asked him to take me somewhere for $5, and he drove me to Coney Island. I got out of the cab. It was 3:00 AM I walked on the boardwalk. I walked on the beach. I walked through empty amusement parks. I walked by Nathan's and could smell the ghosts of a million hot dogs. That was something. Then, when there was no place left to go, I walked out of Coney Island."

"Where did you go?"

"Nowhere. Just walked. I got completely lost. I walked around in circles for several miles, not recognizing anything. Finally, I decided to follow my nose and let it guide me. And at 6:00 AM I found myself back on Flatbush Avenue near Church Street. I was right around the corner from my apartment building. My feet were so tired. God, was I glad to be home."

"The moral of the story?"

"Well, when you want to leave, take a hike. But, on the other hand, all roads lead to home." They both laughed.

The next day George called me for a little instant analysis, as he called it. He described the situation and then said, "You'd think, after three years, we'd be through with all this."

I looked up their files, glanced through them, and discovered the cause of the crisis.

"It's elementary, my dear Watson!"

"God ahead, doc, I'm all ears," he said, making like Bugs Bunny.

"According to my notes, when both you and Martha were three years old, your worlds changed forever. I'm talking siblings, George."

It was true. When George was three, his mom and Frank had a child, his half-brother Michael whom he never accepted. He was always sick and whining, and George hadn't seen him in six years.

When Martha was three, her sister Karen was born, and she resented her so much she tried twice to suffocate her with a pillow. Unsuccessfully, it turned out.

"Are you with me, George?"

"Yes, boss."

"When a younger sibling is born, the first child is never the same. He is no longer the baby. He no longer has the exclusive attention of his parents. He has serious competition, and what's worse, there's no way he can win. In a way, he is thrown out of his special place in the family, replaced, bumped." George could feel his old jealousy stirring.

"Could this create sexual stuff, doc?"

"Sure could. Remember, these patterns are like time bombs planted in your subconscious mind, set to explode on schedule. Three years is three years."

"Shit."

"What?"

"My kid brother was born on Thanksgiving Day."

"There you go."

"So, what do we do?"

"Just be aware of these forces. And heal it with your siblings. Forgive the little buggers."

"Yeah."

"And George, if you're thinking of fucking around . . ."

"I know, don't!"

"No, not don't. Just put yourself in Martha's shoes first."

"But doc, I never wear heels."

They both laughed.

WAY #20: ALL ROADS LEAD TO HOME

The fundamental problem with leaving is that it rarely gets you anywhere. Of course, there are times when leaving is not only advisable, but totally appropriate, such as when you're in a self-destructive relationship, creating abuse, and suddenly you find the self-esteem to say, "No more!" In such cases you must leave to reclaim your own dignity, and prepare for a relationship that reflects more of what you truly deserve.

But the compulsive leaving pattern is more a function of healthy, loving relationships. You just want to leave, split, disappear because you feel the urge to move on. Where are you going? Anywhere. You just need to get away.

Most of us, when we were kids, wanted to run away from home at least once. It is a common fantasy, often acted out. When you grow up, form an adult relationship, settle down, and create a home of your own, your old feeling of being stuck at home again might come up, for no good reason. It's just that home, any home, even your ideal home, reminds you of your parents, your siblings and whatever else you wanted to run away from as a kid. Of course, part of the reason you wanted to run away back then was to make a home of your own. But now you have a home of your own, yet you still feel like running away. . . . It's a vicious cycle.

What's worse, your mind cannot justify leaving when things are good. So you tend to make it bad, mad, or sad in order to have a reason to run. Of course, whatever you leave incomplete or unresolved will follow you. You can and do take it with you.

So take a long walk with yourself. Resolve the feelings you had about wanting to leave home. Make your peace with your siblings. Keep on walking 'til it feels better.

But don't leave. What's the point? All roads lead to home.

AFFIRMATIONS

1. *I'm free to leave an unhealthy relationship.*

2. *I never create an upset just to justify leaving.*

3. *Whenever I create an upset, I know I've set it up for healing.*

4. *I forgive myself for wanting to run away from home.*

5. *I no longer have to run away to be free.*

6. *When I'm free of my past, I'm free to come and go as I please.*

7. *I can stay and move through this.*

8. *This, too, shall pass.*

9. *I love my home more than I love leaving.*

10. *My home is an expression of my freedom.*

11. *I choose to make my home a perfect place to be.*

12. *My relationship is an expression of my freedom.*

13. *I choose to make my relationship a perfect place to be.*

14. *I can leave and come back without ever leaving.*

15. *It's okay to take a break once in a while.*

16. *My purpose in taking a break is greater intimacy, not separation.*

17. *I can take a walk instead of running away.*

18. *It's safe to run towards love.*

19. *I run to the highest thought.*

20. *Since I have a good sense of direction, I always know which way to go.*

—21—

Leave No Stone Unturned

It was January 1, 1970—a new year and a new decade—when George and Martha flew to New York for a visit. The snow began falling in blankets as soon as their United flight landed at JFK. They took a taxi to the Helmsley Palace, where they were shown to a magnificent room overlooking St. Patrick's Cathedral. They made love all evening in their deluxe king-size bed and slept until noon the next day. It was still snowing as they sat up in bed, eating their eggs Benedict.

George wanted to make his peace with his father Frank, who wasn't his real father but still was the only one he had ever known. He knew he had never been fair to either Frank or his brother Michael, unable to let them into his heart out of some insane loyalty to the father whose genes he carried. As a child he perceived Frank, quite mistakenly, as a tyrant, a dictator who had marched in and usurped the position of the rightful ruler. He even would have dreams where Frank was the enemy killing his dad at Pearl Harbor. Of course, all of this was just the concoction of his childish imagination, but he could never face the truth until now. Martha was the one who encouraged him. "He couldn't be that bad," she kept saying, "or else you wouldn't have turned out so good."

It was true. Frank Abrahms was a wonderful man, a short stocky bundle of energy that could not help but be himself. He was a man in love with life—emotional, passionate, brilliant, and a teddy bear to boot. Frank was a real *mensch*. All heart. When he met Elizabeth and her child back in Hawaii during the war, he fell in love for the first time in his life. And without any invitation, he pursued the grieving widow, who reminded him of Katherine Hepburn, until she too fell for him, who reminded her of Spencer Tracy.

Frank was a private detective. He had his own agency and was quite successful. His son Michael was at Columbia Law School. The only sore spot in his heart was George, who had rejected him from day one. Frank was not used to rejection and even less with not being able to figure things out. He blamed himself and carried his failure with George heavily, though he never mentioned it to Elizabeth, who knew anyway.

George called his mother, and she was all tears on the phone. He melted, too, and they could hardly speak. Martha had to take the receiver and tell her they'd be over for dinner at 7:00 PM as they had previously arranged. George got dressed and went out for a walk. Martha watched soap operas.

He drifted aimlessly like the snow. There was a ton of it. Fifth Avenue was a cross-country ski trail and New Yorkers were thoroughly enjoying the whitewash, which had the city at its mercy. He knew where he was going. He wanted to see Frank before dinner. Why postpone the inevitable?

He could feel all his repressed love for Frank, but his mind was still questioning the man, wondering if he was a scoundrel or a marshmallow. As he stood before the huge office building, he knew somehow that Frank would be at his desk, even though the rest of New York was closed down.

He climbed up the stairs to the second floor, not bothering with the elevator. He stopped at the door and read the gold leaf lettering on the glass: Red Eye Detective Agency—"We leave no stone unturned."

George opened the door and walked in. There was a blonde receptionist filing her nails who greeted him. When he asked for Mr. Abrahms, she buzzed one of the inner offices and Frank came right out, all blustery like the day.

"Georgie, how you doing?" He went to hug him. "It's my kid, Mary, the movie star." George's body stiffened up as his father hugged him, much to both their dismay. George was really trying.

"Hi, Frank. Just thought I'd drop by."

"It's good to see you, son. Your series is great. Come in." And he ushered him into his private office, a huge space with a long oak desk, wall-to-wall bookcases, a bar, stereo, and twenty-five-inch Panasonic TV George could see his father was a bigger success than he had imagined.

"A drink, kid?"

"Vodka on the rocks." George decided to have a drink, something he rarely did anymore. It was a special occasion. They sat down, the desk between them, toasted to father and son reunions, then sank into an awkward silence.

"How's Michael?"

"Mike's great. Last year at Columbia Law. Second in his class. He tries harder, you know? A wiz, that kid. Don't know where he gets it from. He wants to work with me when he gets out, but I can't see it. Not with a mind like that. He's got Attorney General written all over him."

"I can't wait to see him."

"Tonight, no?"

"Of course."

"How's Martha?"

"You're gonna love her, Frank. She's one in a million."

"Gotta be to hold on to you this long, eh?" They laughed.

"What exactly do you do here, Frank?"

"Do? As little as possible. No, I'm really very busy here. Detection is booming. Everybody's looking for someone. I've got a special project going now. I'm working with the parents of runaway kids."

"Sounds interesting."

"It's pretty sad. Seems like the whole world is running away from home . . ." Frank stopped in his tracks.

"I've really missed you, son."

George could feel the tears well up. Frank was being amazing.

"I got to apologize. I think I was insensitive when you were a kid."

"You did your best."

"No. I could have done better. I just sort of barged in on your territory and announced I was your father."

"You did a lot for me . . . Dad." He had never called him that before. "I just couldn't let you in." Suddenly, he had reached his limits, he couldn't hold it back, and all there was was tears, sobbing. Frank handed him a tissue and took two for himself.

"We're well stocked with Kleenex here. A lot of fathers and sons cry in this office."

"I never got over my father, Frank."

"I know, George. It must have been hell."

"I never even knew him."

"I wish I could have brought him back to you."

"You were great. You loved Mom so much."

"Still do. Old Kate Hepburn to this day. Only better looking. Wait 'til you see her."

"I had to see you first."

"I appreciate that. I really do."

"I've been looking for myself for so long it finally led me to you."

"That's the way it goes, huh?"

"When you moved in, Frank, it was like I lost a part of myself."

"Maybe I can help you find it."

"You already have."

"Yeah, but I want it all out. All your cards on the table."

"Leave no stone unturned, eh?"

"Smart kid, aren't you?"

WAY #21: LEAVE NO STONE UNTURNED

You can't write off any major influence on your life. You can't sweep a grandmother, stepfather, half-sister, or crazy uncle under the rug and pretend he, or she, never existed. You can try. You can deny. But in the end that person is locked up in your heart forever, or until the day you open up.

Any unresolved past relationship can cause separation in a current one. You might want to leave your partner at the very point you couldn't handle your uncle. Say your uncle was crass and vulgar and whenever your partner cracks a dirty joke, that old embarrassment around your uncle comes up and you want to leave the room. Or maybe it's your sister who used to lose her keys all the time and drive you up the wall. So whenever your partner misplaces his keys, it's your helpless sister all over again. If you don't forgive and forget everyone in your family, you might find the ghosts of all your cousins and your uncles and your aunts moving in with you. Talk about haunted houses.

Step-parents are especially tricky. You might be tempted to dismiss them as unreal. That's ridiculous, of course; they are as real as real parents. They really parented you, and you had a real relationship with them. Still do. Often children will transfer their unresolved anger about a legitimate parent who left onto a step-parent. The real father becomes the good guy, and the stepfather the bad guy, holding the mother for a ransom, as it were. This distortion of reality can become a deeply embedded fantasy, causing a twisted perception of all your intimate relationships.

If in your mind your good parent abandoned you and was replaced by a wicked intruder, you could subconsciously drive a good partner to leave you and replace him or her with a bad one.

Anyone who loved and nurtured you as a child contributed to the wonderful person you've become. Unlock your heart. Open the floodgates.

Leave no stone unturned.

Affirmations

1. I am grateful for all my relatives.
2. I thank everyone who loved me as a child.
3. I am willing to see my past differently.
4. I'd rather forgive than hold grudges.
5. My whole family is a blessing.
6. I forgive myself for taking sides in my family's feuds.
7. I can now see my whole family did the best they could.
8. I forgive myself for withholding love from those who loved me.
9. I forgive myself for shutting my family out.
10. I forgive my family for their unconscious behavior towards me.
11. I forgive everyone I ever let influence me negatively.
12. I forgive myself for allowing myself to be influenced negatively.
13. I am at peace with all my relatives.
14. I am grateful for my entire family.
15. I love my roots.
16. My roots free me to grow.
17. The more I nurture my roots, the more I grow.
18. My whole family tree is a tree of life.
19. I never have to leave my roots to grow.
20. Thank God for my family tree.

—22—

Steer Clear of Bermuda Triangles

George and Martha were drifting off course. Had they been alert, they would have noticed this immediately and made the necessary corrections. Had they been alert, they would have remembered Hana the Kahuna's warning about Bermuda. They would have remembered their karma. They would have asked for forgiveness before they went. Unknown to them, they had been drifting in unconsciousness for almost six months, ever since the trip to New York. On one level they were happy as clams, blissed out in love, even considering marriage, a topic they had avoided since their first few days together. On another level, however, they were completely asleep, blowing with the wind, and about to put their relationship to its ultimate test. Had they been alert they would have remembered all they had learned. And they probably never would have gone to Bermuda in the first place.

It was another family gathering. They were joined by Alex and Sarah, Sally and Beth, Karen and David. They had four adjoining rooms at the Bermuda Palms, overlooking a pure pink sand beach and the turquoise waters of the Atlantic. The first night George and Martha held each other tight and she asked, "Do you think that when we're married we'll still be on a honeymoon?"

"If not, we'll get divorced and start over."

The second night George was walking with Karen on the beach. She was very beautiful in the moonlight, and he was turned on. George was always turned on these days. He blamed it on Martha's new wave of sexual energy. He felt as though a spell had been cast on him.

"You know, George," Karen started, "I'm twenty-two and still a virgin." George found this hard to believe.

"It's true," she added. "Technically speaking."

Karen was the quintessential California fox—tall, sleek, and an angel in a bikini. Surely, guys couldn't keep their hands off her, George was thinking.

"I've had my share of offers, of course."

"Of course."

"But I've held out for the right man."

"You must have very strong willpower."

"I do, very strong." She giggled and took George's hand in hers. The energy raced up and down his body. "I've experimented with girls, you know."

"Me too," he said; and they laughed.

"You know, in some cultures the older sister's husband is required to make it with all the younger sisters."

"Too bad I'm not married."

"Hmmm."

They walked on in silence, brushing against each other. Finally, he stopped and, turning her to him, held and kissed her as he had been wanting to for years.

Martha and David were sitting at the bar, drinking rum punches. She was laughing at his joke about the Jewish American Princess whose favorite sexual position was facing Bloomingdales.

"What's yours?" he asked.

"My what, David?" She smiled seductively. She enjoyed his attention. This was no negative reflection on George. George was a perfect George, David a perfect David. And at this point in her life, Martha felt a deep need to have them both! The truth was, her sexual appetite was unmanageable these days. She was turned on by everyone—young boys, older men, and David Levy. She was even turned on by the ocean, moonlight, and the rum punches didn't hurt either. George, for his part, had done his best to satisfy her, but the more he made love to her the more love she wanted to make. She didn't understand it. She didn't even approve of it. But when you're spinning in a tornado of sexual energy, you can't just snap your fingers and calm the storm. You ride it out. At least, that's the way Martha was thinking.

"Actually, David," she finally answered, "I like to experiment." David knew they had reached that familiar point in their relationship, that border between innocent flirtation and real romance. And once again he didn't know which he wanted. His friendship with George was extremely important to him. So was his desire for Martha.

"George and I have an open relationship, you know."

"No, I didn't."

"We've never actually done anything, but George insisted from the start that greater openness leads to greater closeness."

"Interesting theory."

"So I'm free as a bird, David."

"How do birds do it?"

"In midair, I think." They laughed. She reached under the table and stroked him.

Alex and Sarah couldn't figure out who the girls were with that week. Only Sally seemed stable in her love for Beth. Sarah kept urging her husband to speak to the kids, but he was reluctant. Finally, one day he found himself alone with George at the pool bar.

"So, George, how do you like Bermuda?"

"It's like a drug, Alex. I'm on some far-out trip."

"You mean Karen?"

"Yes."

"And Martha and David?"

"It's utterly insane, Alex. But we're trying to let it be."

"All in the family anyway."

"I guess it's hard to watch go down."

"I'm not the voyeur type, George."

They drank their beers and watched the waterfalls send miniature rainbows skipping across the pool.

"I guess I'm just old-fashioned, George. I never could fool around. I had plenty of opportunity, I'll admit, and a few close calls. But in the end, it just never felt right."

"I guess we're just different."

"It's a different age. Everyone's betraying someone."

"I'm not betraying Martha. Or she me."

"Maybe you're right, son. I don't know. The important thing is that neither of you betray yourself."

George thought about that for a long time. He didn't feel as though he were betraying himself, but, then again, maybe he did and didn't know it. What does it feel like to betray yourself anyway? You could be having the greatest time of your life and, at the same time, be ripping yourself off entirely. You could be happy in the moment and, unknown to you, be a moment away from disaster. Or could you?

His eyes were glued to one particular rainbow under the waterfalls, and suddenly he felt lightheaded. He took a few deep breaths and it was then he remembered Hana the Kahuna's warning. Suddenly, all his euphoria vanished. He was back in his body. It felt like a jolt of electricity. Like someone turned the light on in his mind. He was fully conscious for the first time in months. And he knew what a Bermuda Triangle felt like.

Martha, meanwhile, was in bed with David, who was passionately thrusting into her. She wasn't really there and her eyes drifted to a palm tree outside the window. She thought she saw their guardian angel waving a finger at her. Then she, too, remembered Hana and started weeping uncontrollably.

"Oh God, forgive me. Please forgive me. Forgive us both. Forgive all of us."

WAY #22: STEER CLEAR OF BERMUDA TRIANGLES

Lyle Watson says "incest" is the only dirty word in the English dictionary. He could be right. The "incest taboo" is the unspoken dirty joke in every family's closet. Not that it's acted out regularly. But the thoughts and feelings are fairly universal. A son wants his mother for himself, thinks he'd make a better husband than his dad, dreams about replacing him. A daughter wants to feel her father's touch, fantasizes about sleeping with him. These are natural feelings and fantasies, part of the evolution into sexual maturity, part of growing up sexual. To clamp a lid on these feelings is to repress your sexuality, and whatever is repressed will rear its mischievous little head in mysterious little ways. Or not so little.

Such as triangles. We create triangles as adults, torn between two lovers, because, as children, we're torn between our love for one parent and our desire for the other. The mind thrives on familiar situations. What it remembers is a triangle, and what it creates is a triangle.

We all seem to have an intimacy threshold. When you get too close to one person, you automatically shut down, withdraw, go unconscious, or gravitate towards someone else. Or you pull in a third party for your mate, and then feel excluded the way you did as a child from your parents' relationship. Or when a younger sibling stole your daddy's, or mommy's, heart from you.

The point at which you could not get any closer to your mother or father defines the point at which you drift away from your partner. It could have been when your dad wouldn't let you sit on his lap any more, or your mom wouldn't tuck you in at night. If your parents did not explain their actions to your satisfaction, you might have become confused, guilty, or resentful. You might have thought there was something wrong with you as a woman or man to cause such abrupt rejection. You might have concluded that your sexuality was bad or dirty or unattractive. You may still feel that way. If so, it could drive you off course, causing you to behave unconsciously. You could even pull away from your lover, or drive him away, without knowing it. Without him knowing it.

You never betray anyone but yourself. And when you betray yourself, you betray everyone you love. If this comes up in your relationship, use it as an opportunity to complete your early sexual confusions, as well as to choose your current relationship more fully. Whatever comes up is on its way out. You set it up so you can understand yourself more, let go of old hurt, and be free to have the love you now deserve.

So, steer clear of Bermuda Triangles. And when you find yourself in one, pray for release.

AFFIRMATIONS

1. *I am no longer threatened by intimacy.*

2. *It's safe to surpass my intimacy threshold.*

3. *I forgive my mother for withdrawing physically.*

4. *I forgive my father for withdrawing physically.*

5. *I no longer come between people in order to find love.*

6. *My love never causes separation.*

7. *It's safe to put all my eggs in one basket.*

8. *I can have it all in one relationship.*

9. *There are no limits to the sexual bliss I can enjoy with my partner.*

10. *I never have to divide myself in order to feel whole.*

11. *I forgive my younger siblings for stealing my parents' love.*

12. *In sex I'm motivated by love, not power.*

13. *In sex my desire is surrender, not control.*

14. *I never use one person to create separation from another.*

15. *It's safe to be with one person 100%.*

16. *My relationship is off limits to third parties.*

17. *When I'm true to myself, I'm true to my relationship.*

18. *When my eyes wander, my mind is clear.*

19. *I am only seduced by what nurtures me deeply.*

20. *I make love in my body, not in my mind.*

—23—

Marry Yourself First

George and Martha recovered from their Bermuda flings with renewed commitment, fresh energy, and clear that they wanted to get married. They planned their wedding for Thanksgiving Day, which was already their anniversary. Karen finally fell in love and so did David Levy, and it was with each other, and that seemed perfect to all concerned.

George and Martha returned to the simple spiritual practices that seemed to ground their relationship—meditation, yoga, chanting, and silence. They now knew they both had a tendency towards upwards displacement, as they called it, and that spirituality, for them, was a matter of keeping their feet on the planet while their minds explored other realities.

Martha thought of it first, and when she told George, he liked the idea. They called me both to invite me to the wedding and to get my opinion on Martha's new idea, which I found intriguing. They also called Hana, first to ask her if she'd marry them and, second, to ask her what she thought. She told them it was a great idea, and thought all couples should do it before getting married.

So they did it, their own program of premarital rites culminating with Martha's brilliant idea. For three months they ate no meat, drank no alcohol, were celibate and practiced their marital vows. And on the weekend before the wedding, they put Martha's plan into action.

The idea was this: each would do a three-day isolation experience. The rules were simple. Each would lock himself in a cabin somewhere and not go outside. There would be no distractions—no reading, writing, TV, radio, stereo. No nothing. And no sneaking walks in the woods.

George drove up to the Sierras and found a deserted old mining shack, which he decided would do just fine. There was one room, a cot with a sagging mattress, and a wood-burning stove that worked. He parked his car by the mine entrance, unloaded his minimal food supplies, gathered some wood, and locked himself in.

At first he was restless beyond belief. He paced back and forth for forty-five minutes, wanting to leave. He lay down on the cot and tried to relax, but the bumps in the mattress felt like rocks, and he got up and paced again. He felt all this energy rushing through him. He broke out in a cold sweat. His throat itched terribly. He developed a wicked cough. He had to get out. He couldn't take it. At one point he actually opened the door and almost walked out, but, at the last second, he slammed the door shut, determined to stick it out no matter what, to face himself fully, to confront whatever dark shadows loomed in his unconsciousness, and to overcome his fear of staying put.

After three hours of solitude George was exhausted and fell asleep on the hardwood floor. He had some very interesting dreams. In one, a crazy old hag was chasing him through the woods with an axe. "I'm sorry! I'm sorry!" he heard himself scream, and suddenly it was raining, raining so hard the woods transformed into a rain forest. And the witch was dissolving, turning into another being, and this new being was their golden guardian angel, smiling as the axe became a magic wand she waved over him.

In another dream he was visiting Frank's office, only the words on the glass door were different, "Red Eye of Love." When George entered, Frank and Martha were making it on the floor, and then it was Frank and his mother Elizabeth, and then it was not Frank at all but another man, in a Navy uniform, his father. Frank was standing next to him now, arm around the boy, "You see, son, I told you. We specialize in happy reunions."

Martha drove to a cabin near Palm Springs. It was an unusually hot day, and she was sweating when she locked herself in. She was immediately hungry and busied herself in the little country kitchen, preparing some shrimp salad on pita bread. She put together her sandwich, poured blue cheese dressing over it, and devoured it with a Perrier as she watched the pink and purple sunset over the craggy desert mountains. She thought of George, up there somewhere.

She unpacked her suitcase on the bear rug in front of the stone fireplace, then went into the bedroom and lay down on the big cozy old oak four-poster bed, where she breathed for twenty minutes. This was not bad, she thought, not half bad. Three days here would be a welcome vacation. Thank you, Sally and Beth, whose cabin it was.

Martha fell asleep and immediately dreamed about giving birth. She was in a warm pool somewhere, maybe Hawaii. Hana was there, which was why she thought Hawaii. And George was supporting her. She could see herself totally relaxed in his arms, reclining with her legs spread as Hana prayed in silence. There were glowing green mountains and meadows all around, and the night sky was full of bright stars. She could make out Orion. There was music, and she looked up, and the guardian angel was playing the harp. Then the baby came out, a boy, a beautiful bright blue-eyed boy, and the birth itself was simple, easy, painless, just one long rush of release. Hana was holding the baby, telling her that he was a special being, with a special purpose. Martha held the baby to her bosom. She sobbed tears of joy. It was a picture postcard scene, this birth of her dreams.

The second and third days were easier for George. He paced a lot and recited thirty Shakespeare sonnets, which were all he could remember. He thought about Martha and wondered if he'd ever figure her out. Hot, cold, light, dark, soft, tough, bubbly, still. . . . Where she goes, nobody knows.

He played the flute for hours, which maybe was against the rules, but so what? Rules were meant to be broken, and flutes to be tooted. Although he couldn't see them, he could hear a chorus of birds singing along. He felt like the Pied Piper and thought it would be a great role to play.

Martha thought she bilocated the second day. She was sitting on the bear rug in front of the fireplace, meditating. Before she knew it, she was sitting on the hardwood floor next to George in a shack. He was playing his flute and the birds were singing.

George felt a presence and shuddered. He put down his flute and started sniffing. He could smell Martha's rose oil perfume. He looked around and then saw her, her form, like a ghost of herself, sitting beside him. He wanted to hug her but knew she wasn't real except in his mind. (He would later find out the truth.) "I love you," he said, and she blew him a kiss and disappeared into thin air. The birds were still chirping.

The last night they both had the same dream. A wedding. Bells everywhere. A huge cathedral. The Mormon Tabernacle Choir singing the "Hallelujah Chorus." Hana the Kahuna performing the ceremony. Alex and Sarah Kaplan, proud as can be. Frank and Elizabeth Abrahms crying for joy. Their guardian angel, hanging from the chandelier, throwing confetti.

Both their dreams were identical except for one thing. In George's dream, when he turned to see the bride, it was himself. In Martha's dream, the groom she faced was herself.

When they drove home the next day, their timing was uncanny. They almost collided head-on turning into the driveway, so eager were they to reunite. They leapt out of their cars and embraced, while traffic backed up along their street. Horns started honking and they turned and saw and laughed.

They were truly connected now. Married to themselves, there seemed to be much more of them available to each other. As though their very presence took up more space. Nor had they ever been so intimate. And without sex, they realized that intimacy was something they had never really known. Now it was there, a feeling, an openness, a sense of deep touch.

Their premarital rites were complete.

Way #23: Marry Yourself First

Before you get married, marry yourself. Prepare yourself for marital bliss way in advance. Take yourself by your own hand, lead yourself to the altar, give yourself away to yourself in the presence of yourself, and take yourself, for better or worse, through good times and bad, in sick-

ness and health, now and forever, so help you, God! Now give yourself
a hug.

If you are not committed to your own joy and well-being, who else
will be? If you are not willing to stick it out with yourself, can you blame
others for leaving? People relate to you the way you relate to yourself.
If you're stuck on a blind date with yourself and can't wait until it's over,
do you honestly expect anyone else to enjoy your company? A marriage
just reflects the state of the union within each of the partners. If you're
all fragmented, of course your relationship will fall to pieces. There's no
one else out there, you know. Just you and the mirror.

So lock yourself in a room with yourself for a few days. No distractions. Wrestle with your own demons, devils, and dark shadows. And
don't give up until you make your peace with each of them, resolving
your own inner conflicts. Stop running away from your hidden self. It's
a race you cannot win.

All too often, we're afraid of being alone. We ricochet from one casual affair to another, trying hopelessly to find temporary buffers from
the emptiness we think we cannot face. No one can fill that emptiness
but you. The spring flows from within. But if you're afraid of being
alone, you'll never find this out. You'll always look for another source
outside yourself. Until you enter the woods and feel the solitude of your
soul, you're stuck alone. You can fantasize about a knight on a white
horse coming along to save you, rescue you, and swoop you off in his
arms, but when you open your eyes, you'll still be by yourself. Until
you're alone, you're with no one.

And what's to be rescued from? Underneath all your fear, behind
the dark curtain, beyond the black shadow—there you stand in bright
light, in all your glory, radiance, and magnificence. Is it your own "god-
likeness" you shy away from?

Every culture has its rites of passage, initiations. So take the bull by
the horns. Slay the dragon. Kill the beast.

Or else you'll always be a shadow of yourself.

Affirmations

1. My commitment to myself is my first priority.
2. My relationships support my commitment to myself.
3. I am willing to marry myself.
4. I am my perfect partner.
5. It's safe knowing me.
6. It's safe facing my fear.
7. It's safe to be alone.
8. I no longer run away when I'm lonely.
9. I no longer expect my partner to make me whole.
10. I am the source.
11. I no longer deny myself.
12. I accept myself fully.
13. I love myself unconditionally.
14. When I embrace my dark side, I create more light.
15. Even my dark side nourishes me.
16. My light and dark sides are one.
17. I can survive without internal conflict.
18. I no longer need to suppress my fears to survive.
19. I'm safe when I'm afraid.
20. In my defenselessness my safety lies.

—24—

Have a Common Sense
of Humor

The night before their wedding was a nasty one. They went out to Luigi's for Italian food, and the rain was blowing so hard it turned George's umbrella inside out. Martha was laughing when they sat down at a table and ordered antipasta. Later, they were eating spaghetti bolognese when they both broke out laughing.

"What's the difference between a Jewish American Princess and spaghetti?" Martha said, her mouth half full.

"Spaghetti moves when you eat it," George completed the old joke, practically choking.

"That's disgusting," she said.

"I know."

They couldn't stop laughing at the stupid joke. And then it wasn't even the joke they were laughing at, it was simply the fact that they were laughing. And it was everything. Themselves. The world.

A middle-aged, married couple was sitting at a table across from them. He was bald, fat, and smoking a thick cigar. She was a small, spunky, pull-up-your-sleeves-and-handle-it type of woman. They weren't very happy. The man was kvetching, blaming his wife for their daughter's alleged lack of respect. The woman was defending the accused as a normal teenager.

"Normal? Normal?" he cried. "You call it normal to shave your head and smoke cigars? Who the hell does she think she is? Kojak?" And he puffed cigar smoke rings, three at a time in her face.

George and Martha couldn't contain themselves. They found the conversation incredibly funny. Their laughter consumed them. The man turned on them, glaring. And just then, just when the man was about to say something he didn't want to say and they didn't want to hear, just then, at the perfect moment, a waiter tripped on an ice cube, sliding to the floor and dropping a huge plate of fettucine alfredo in the man's lap.

The man sprang to action at once, leaping to his feet, pushing the poor waiter away, and storming out of the restaurant into the pouring rain, with no coat or hat, shouting, "I never get any respect!"

George, Martha, and the abandoned wife were all laughing. The waiter was climbing off the floor, the manager hovering over him, arms akimbo. And then the sprinkler system went, flooding the whole restaurant, and George opened his umbrella, nonchalantly guiding a giddy Martha out.

They were still laughing in the car. They decided to go see a Marx Brothers double feature, *Duck Soup* and *Monkey Business*, two of their all-time favorites. George was telling her why Groucho's show, "You Bet Your Life," had been cancelled.

"This guy, one of the contestants, says he's got thirteen kids or something. Groucho says, 'Isn't that excessive?' The guy says he likes kids. Groucho says he likes his cigar, but he takes it out of his mouth once in a while."

Martha loved it. She guffawed. They laughed so much, their ribs ached.

When they got home, after the movies, they were really horny. It was their last night of celibacy, and they considered cheating but decided not to. They couldn't decide what to do with their energy. So they turned on a rerun of "The Honeymooners" and laughed at the antics of Ralph, Alice, and Norton. Then they watched *The Great Dictator*, where Charlie Chaplin as Adolf Hitler dances with the globe like a beach ball. They laughed all through the night.

At dawn they got up and walked on the beach, one last time as single folk. It was foggy, damp, and romantic—like the setting of an English novel. They walked hand-in-hand. They kissed tenderly. He was wearing a trench coat with nothing underneath, she a yellow slicker. Suddenly, in the middle of a kiss, Martha broke out laughing again. George, feeling the humor of the night before resurface, laughed too.

"What's so funny?" George asked.

"I forgot the keys."

Neither of them had keys. George never had keys. She never forgot them. Except now. Their wedding ceremony was in two hours. George said, not to worry, he'd break in through the bathroom window. He gave it a good try, smashing the glass with an elbow, then climbing up to the ledge. As he was in the middle of climbing in, however, half-exposed, half-trench coat, a police car siren sounded, and George turned to look.

The headlights caught him in the act. Never mind that it was the act of breaking into his own home. In this case the image was the message, and George knew he was caught in a compromising position. The cop got out of the car, pulled a gun, and booked them both on breaking and entering, unlawful entry, and questionable apparel, if there is such a thing.

They were laughing too hard to defend themselves. Did you hear the one about the Jewish American Princess who got arrested for indecent exposure on her wedding day? While practicing celibacy?

Way #24: Have a Common Sense of Humor

It is now common knowledge that humor is healing. "Laughter therapy" has been used successfully in curing even terminally ill patients. So we should never underestimate the seriousness of taking things lightly.

Especially ourselves. And our relationships. The ability to lighten up is the first step towards enlightenment, and without that single step, your whole journey could become meaningless. Or meaningful. You may think it's hard to laugh at yourself, your problems, the woes of the world. You may think pain and suffering are more warranted. But when you add more negative mass to the pain there already is, you just dig a deeper hole to climb out of, with more weight on your shoulders. You could even bury yourself alive. Looking at life as a divine comedy is a definite alternative. Worth considering.

Having a common sense of humor with your partner is an enormous asset to your relationship. It can lift your spirits when things seem most bleak. Let's face it, when you're with someone who never laughs when you do, it can get pretty discouraging. Imagine watching a movie like Some Like It Hot, or The Producers *with a partner who sat there stone-faced the entire time. Pretty sad, huh? It's one thing to have differences of opinion in your relationship, it's quite another to have different world views entirely.*

Your sense of humor is, in effect, your frame of reference, the way you look at life itself. A comic perspective is an optimistic world view. The belief that everything's going down the tubes, there's nothing anyone can do about it, is tragic and does not serve the longevity of any relationship. In fact, it could send you and your partner down the tubes, too.

The mask of tragedy has no business on a lover's face. It's comedy that creates resolution in our lives.

Never miss a good excuse to laugh. And when your partner's laughing, try to see things his way. Or hers.

AFFIRMATIONS

1. *I never take myself too seriously.*

2. *I never take life too personally.*

3. *I am always willing to see the light side of things.*

4. *Even when things get heavy, I'm willing to see the humor.*

5. *I love to laugh.*

6. *I love a good joke.*

7. *Even when the joke's on me, I can laugh.*

8. *My partner and I love to laugh together.*

9. *The more we laugh, the more we love.*

10. *The more we love, the more we laugh.*

11. *People are funny.*

12. *My problems may be jokes in disguise.*

13. *I can laugh at my leaving pattern.*

14. *Every cloud has a funny lining.*

15. *I have compassion even when I laugh at someone.*

16. *People can laugh at me and still be loving me.*

17. *Whenever I laugh, I let go and live more.*

18. *Whenever I laugh, my heart opens more.*

19. *Laughter is healthy to my mind and body.*

20. *I never miss an opportunity to laugh.*

— 25 —

For Whom the Bells
Rock and Roll

Martha loved bells. Always had. As a kid she started collecting them—clay bells, crystal bells, silver bells, porcelain bells, cow bells, china bells, little bells, big bells. Once, when she was three, her mom showed her a picture of the Liberty Bell in a history book, and she cried for the crack for an hour. She loved Soleri bells, several of which hung in the house and on the deck, church bells, Christmas bells and, most of all, she loved wedding bells. Alex Kaplan used to call his little daughter "The Bell of Beverly Hills." In school the kids called her "Ding-a-ling."

She had a dream that when she got married, all the bells of Los Angeles would ring at once so the whole world would know how happy she was. Alex Kaplan liked this idea. He liked it when his kids thought big. And, being a powerful and influential man, he made the necessary arrangements. On Thanksgiving Day, 1970, at his kid's wedding, all the bells he could find would ring. So the whole world would know how happy she was.

George and Martha, having convinced the police sergeant that they were who they claimed to be and that this was their wedding day, received a police escort back to their house to dress, and then on to a private club in Beverly Hills, where the wedding was. They raced through the streets of L.A. at 100 MPH, the police siren clearing the way. They still couldn't stop laughing. A police escort to their own wedding! When they stopped in front of the club, it was exactly 10:00 AM, and all those church bells started ringing, and Martha's laughter turned to tears of joy. She stood on the steps, George's arm around her, weeping because she was so moved. Her childhood dream was now a reality. She was sure that so many bells had never rung together before, and she closed her eyes and remembered the first bell she ever heard—the Good Humor Man who had a shiny steel bell on the side of his truck; when he rang it all the kids would come running.

George held her to him as they laughed and cried. A bell was ringing in his head, too. He was remembering Mrs. Winter, his second grade teacher, who started class every morning by ringing a small china bell, which would signal the class to rise and sing "America." The song was going through his mind now,

> *America, America,*
> *God shed His grace on thee,*
> *And crown thy good with brotherhood*
> *From sea to shining sea.*

The wedding was sensational. Everyone who was anyone was there, and George and Martha were the superstars. When they entered the ballroom, everyone cheered, and a band played "Silver Bells," and all three hundred people took out the tiny glass bells Alex had given them and rang them together. Martha was overwhelmed with feeling.

Hana the Kahuna performed the ceremony, which was short and sweet. She told them they had been married for many lifetimes so this ceremony was a little redundant. Everyone laughed. She told them their karma was clear, and all the bells meant grace and redemption. She said that she could not marry them 'til death do them part because they could die a thousand times and still would never part. And, besides, maybe they would never die. She winked at them. She told them that they were the only ones who could marry each other, and she was just the witness. They were the priest and priestess, and they should now bow before each other, which they did as the whole crowd meditated in silence for two minutes. Then George told Martha, "I love you and will never leave you," and Martha told George, "I love you and will never leave you." And they exchanged rings. Then Hana did the Peace of I blessing, after which she handed Martha an old gold kahuna bell, which she said was 5,000 years old and would bless them for eternity. When Martha rang the bell, the sound was so pure and ancient it seemed like the whole room was transformed in one holy instant.

And then George and Martha kissed, and everyone cheered. And all the bells rang. And everyone hugged everyone. And the band played, "I Want to Hold Your Hand," and everyone danced all day and night.

George and Martha would never forget their wedding day. But there was one moment above all others that would stand out in their memory. They were about to go upstairs to their honeymoon suite and they turned back for one last look at the party nobody wanted to end. The band was playing another Beatles' song,

> *Bright are the stars that shine,*
> *Dark is the sky,*
> *I know this love of mine*
> *Will never die,*
> *And I love her . . .*

Everyone was dancing cheek-to-cheek. They both saw it at the same time, the golden cloud surrounding the huge chandelier. And there in the middle of the cloud sat their guardian angel, smiling and ringing a bell, too.

Way #25: For Whom the Bells Rock and Roll

When you get married, make certain the wedding is a celebration of what is, not a promise of what can never be.

A wedding is ideally the public exposure of a private union. It is the ultimate acknowledgment of two hearts becoming one. It is a holy and sacred moment as well as a time to celebrate love and renew life.

Too many people get married for the wrong reasons. They marry out of insecurity, hope, fantasy, expectation. A wedding is not a magic wand that will make a bad relationship good, or a good one better. And it is not a free ticket to clear sailing. There is no ceremony that will insure your future. No ritual to make you other than who you are. So let your wedding be a reflection of the perfection you already feel, not a projection of false hope and impossible fantasy.

Create your own wedding ceremony. Let it be an expression of your higher selves, your gratitude, your innocence, your joy and aliveness. For who can marry you but you? Who is the higher authority you would give your power to? A church? A judge? There's no one. It's the God in each of you who come together. Let this God and Goddess say the vows as they announce publicly, here and now on planet Earth, what is already a fact of life in heaven. And let the bells ring, resonate, resound, and rock and roll. For you!

AFFIRMATIONS

1. *I have no illusions about marriage.*

2. *The reality of love is better than any fantasy.*

3. *Marriage can't change me; I'm already perfect.*

4. *My wedding demonstrates my perfection.*

5. *When I marry, I rejoice.*

6. *My relationship is holy.*

7. *My relationship is blessed.*

8. *My relationship is innocent.*

9. *My relationship is pure.*

10. *My wedding affirms the immortality of my love.*

11. *My wedding inspires others.*

12. *My wedding is a way I share my relationship with the world.*

13. *My marriage is a gift I share with the world.*

14. *My wedding vows reflect my commitment to myself.*

15. *My wedding vows are my heart's desires.*

16. *My wedding is an expression of heaven-on-earth.*

17. *My wedding adds energy to my highest thoughts.*

18. *I can have my ideal wedding.*

19. *I can have my ideal marriage.*

20. *Thank God for my ideal loving relationship.*

—26—

Don't Let What's Not Up Get You Down

It can happen to the best of men. It can happen any time. It just so happened that it happened to George on his wedding night.

It could have been all he had to drink, after not drinking for three months. It could have been that he hadn't slept in 48 hours. It could have been God's little joke on him. It could have been anything. Whatever it was, however, the fact of it was that George just couldn't get it up.

It had never happened before. It might never happen again. But when it happened, and neither George nor Martha could get the little fellow to dance, George went absolutely bonkers. He cried and he screamed and he pounded the walls so hard the people in the next room called the security guard who knocked on the door to find out what was going on.

"Just a bad dream," said Martha, which seemed to satisfy Security.

"It's over! The end! Finis!" George cried when she shut the door. Martha thought it was all hysterically funny. Funnier than going to the police station even. Funnier than the couple at Luigi's. Funnier than all the J.A.P. jokes rolled into one. George just looked so damn funny, stomping and carrying on like some macho man gone amok. Only George wasn't laughing. He was raving.

"It's a curse," he decided. "Someone somewhere is sticking pins in a little George doll, sticking pins in this little doll's cock. I know it. I can feel it."

"Pins in your cock? Ouch." Martha was beside herself.

"Don't be facetious!" he shouted.

"It's funny, George."

"It's over, Martha. You know it. I know it. Let's face it like grown-ups!"

"Maybe it was all those bells."

"Yeah, every bell in the city rings except mine." She laughed. "It's *not* funny!"

"I forgot."

"I knew marriage was a mistake. We were so happy, Martha. Why did we have to ruin a good thing by being normal?"

"George, don't you think you're being a little melodramatic?"

"No! Yes! I can be anyfuckingthing I want to be!"

"I know, George."

"Don't fuck with my mind, Martha."

"I'll take what I can get."

"Very funny. *Very* funny."

George was pacing back and forth, naked, waving his hands wildly in the air. Martha was relaxed on the bed, her luscious body glowing from the moonlight streaming in through the curtains.

"Why me?" he wallowed. "Why me?"

"It's normal, George."

"That's what I hate about it. I don't want to be fucking normal!"

"You're not, George. You'll never be normal."

"You just *said* I'm normal!"

"I said *it's* normal."

He stopped pacing in front of her. He lifted his sleeping organ and screamed at it.

"Don't be so *fucking* normal!"

"Shhh," whispered Martha. "We don't want Security knocking."

"I don't want security! I want *sex*!"

"Your mind wants sex. Your body wants sleep."

"Martha?" he sat down on the bed.

"What, baby?" She stroked his back.

"What if the little bugger never wakes up? I mean, seriously, what if I'm allergic to marriage and my cock has a permanent case of sleeping sickness?"

"Don't worry, George. Princess Charming will provide the magic kiss." She kissed him from behind and held him in her arms, rocking him gently, then pulling him down so they lay there like spoons.

"What's the matter with me? I'm only 29. Too young for a midlife crisis."

"You're cute." She rocked him. He was dozing off.

"It's just my male ego," he mumbled.

"I love your male ego."

"I don't want to be normal. I want to make love. . . ."

"Sure you do."

"I want to. . . ." He was asleep. Like a log.

Martha giggled. She looked at his outstretched body and thought he was Adonis. She loved him so much. She quietly crawled between his spread legs and bent over and kissed his sleeping penis, which stirred, though George didn't.

George was dreaming. He was in the desert watching a huge snake slither. It came right up to him, stretched up off the ground and looked at him, square in the eye. George was staring at this snake which seemed to be smiling at him. Then the face of the snake became Martha's face. She stuck out her tongue at him, and he backed off. Then the snake with Martha's face stood all the way up and looked like an arrow. Then it was a rocket. Then, all of a sudden, it blasted off into the universe.

WAY #26: DON'T LET WHAT'S NOT UP GET YOU DOWN

When you're hot, you're hot, when you're not, you're not! That's what Werner Erhard said about sex, and it makes sense. It also applies to life in general.

When things aren't going the way you like, you can go the way they are going. You can change direction. Life can't. When you're sailing, it's far easier to come about than try to change the wind. People get headstrong in life when they don't get their way—with sex, money, relationships. But your way may not be the way. So let go. Surrender. It's a lot easier than banging your head against the wall.

The ego wants to play God, wants to control, wants to push all the buttons and run the whole show. So when your buttons are pushed, it's a sign that there is another Presence in charge. It's a sign to go with the flow. You might not like the way the roller coaster is going. But don't get off in the middle of the ride.

When you're hot, you seem to be on a roll. Your desires seem to be manifesting instantly. Sex is great. The money's rolling in. Everything's going your way. You feel like it could go on like this forever. Expanding infinitely.

But part of growth is contraction, when you turn inwards, integrate, hibernate, prepare for the next phase of expansion. The whole universe is pulsating all the time, and what is the pulse of life but expansion and contraction? Like a heartbeat. Both phases are necessary. Or else you'd explode or implode. You want balance.

So when you can't get it up, whatever it may be, don't let it get you down. Don't let what's not there be a problem. If it's not there, it's not a problem. And settling into what is there will prove infinitely more satisfying.

Affirmations

1. *I ride life in the direction it's going.*

2. *I surrender to God's perfect plan.*

3. *I am no longer competing with God.*

4. *I am willing for my ego to lose to God.*

5. *I no longer make mountains out of molehills.*

6. *I accept life's ups and downs.*

7. *I can be up, even when things are down.*

8. *I am centered even when things are spinning.*

9. *I am not attached to results.*

10. *I can be satisfied no matter what the results.*

11. *I have nothing to prove sexually.*

12. *I don't have to perform sexually in order to earn love.*

13. *My sexuality is always perfect.*

14. *I am a sexy person.*

15. *I am sexy whether I'm in the mood or not.*

16. *I am sexually innocent.*

17. *I love myself regardless of my sexual mood.*

18. *I have access to unlimited sexual energy.*

19. *I can be intimate with or without sex.*

20. *I am a fabulous lover.*

—27—

You Can Check Out Any Time You Want

The honeymoon continued, and George continued to go crazy, off and on.

They flew from L.A. to London, where they stayed at the Dorchester and took high tea. Martha loved the British elegance. George was damp, cold, and cranky. He started sneezing. They checked out after three days.

They flew to Paris and stayed at the George V. Martha said she felt like a queen or a French whore, she couldn't decide which. George was coughing heavily and complaining about the French attitude towards Americans.

"They act as though they have an exclusive right to good taste. Even if they do, they could at least have the good taste not to flaunt it."

They checked out after two days. They flew from Paris to Athens to Crete, where they stayed in an old Venetian house near the port in Hania. It was hot even though it was December, and the sun felt good to their skin. Even George loved it. Except for the asthma attacks, which were something new and scared him. A Greek doctor told him it was nerves, that he should relax and drink Metoxa. George told him he should stick to medicine.

He was rapidly becoming a hypochondriac. He kept adding new ailments, such as the rash on his belly button, to his repertoire. Secretly, he really believed he was allergic to marriage. Martha just couldn't take it seriously. One day they were sitting at a taverna, sipping retsina and watching a rose sun set into the very blue Aegean.

"This is heaven," she said.

"I'm dead."

"Oh, George."

"If you loved me, you'd let me leave."

"You can leave."

"How can you say that?"

"I love you."

"If you loved me, you'd never let me leave."

"Look at the sunset, George."

George was looking at it all right. And he was thinking it was a sign of the end of his marriage. Tears actually fell from his eyes. Well, at least it would end with some Hollywood flair, not some dumb bang or a whimper. Six days, he was thinking. Six fucking days they had been married. Everything was so fast these days. Six-day wars, six day marriages.

"Six days," he said aloud.

"Tomorrow we can rest," she replied.

Tomorrow I'm splitting, George was thinking. If George had thought about it some more, or called me, he would have remembered that his basic leaving pattern was up, that his father had been killed six days after marrying his mom, and that this six day timetable was etched in stone in his subconscious mind. Somehow he had marriage and death wired together, and his circuits were confused. Which was why he was so nuts.

So they checked out. They flew to Martinique in the Caribbean where George lost his voice and Martha thanked God. He was wheezing like a tea kettle. They'd lie on the beach in absolute silence except for his whistling breath. She tried not to laugh, but it was hard. In her mind none of this was serious. She was certain they'd get through it. Her commitment was strong, and she knew, deep down inside, his was too. He seemed to be testing her, trying every trick in the book to push her away. But the more he pushed, the more she was there. Even George had to admit, she wasn't going anywhere. Nor was he. How could he? Every time he left, she came with him. Besides, anyone who could put up with him when he was so utterly impossible was well worth holding on to. What would he do without her? Survive, his mind said, but his heart knew better. God how he tried to hate her!

One day they were lying on the beach and George whispered hoarsely in her ear, "Is it over yet?"

"What?"

"Life."

"No, George. It's still the first act."

"Is there an intermission?"

She laughed. They checked out the next day and flew to the Yucatan, where they stayed at El Presidente on Cozumel. They flew on a small cigar-shaped plane to Chichen Itza and George felt better among the ruins.

"Maybe you were Mayan in a past life."

"Maybe I'm just a walking ruin come home."

They went to Tulum and made love in an ancient temple facing the sea. George was feeling more himself. The moon was full and they lay on the cool stones, star-gazing.

"I love you, George."

"I hate you, Martha."

"I know." They laughed together.

"I guess we're stuck with each other, huh?"

"Yeah," she said. "Welcome to the Hotel California."

And they both sang the line they were thinking of:

> *You can check out any time you want,*
> *But you can never leave . . .*

WAY #27: YOU CAN CHECK OUT ANY TIME YOU WANT

When you're committed to someone you love, that commitment feels like the strongest pull in your heart, not like an obligation. In fact, to the extent that you feel obligated, you have not yet discovered your real commitment. The bottom line is, when you follow your heart, you honor your commitments. Sometimes it might look crazy. Sometimes it might feel totally impossible. But when you let yourself be yourself, your commitments to those you love deepen.

Sometimes other forces seem to intrude. Sometimes these other forces seem to pull you away from your partner. This is a temporary discrepancy. The truth is, you can never leave those you love when you follow your heart. You might check out once in a while, but you can never leave.

When you follow your intuition, you free yourself to be yourself. You can be your whole self, the good, the bad, the ugly, and the beautiful. And when you're with a partner who gives you the space to be your whole self, without taking it personally or judging the way it looks, you only love him, or her, more. Someone once said, a friend is a person who knows everything about you and loves you anyway. An ideal mate is a friend whose passion for you increases the more he, or she, experiences your diversity.

We're all complex beings. We have multiple personalities. We're chameleons. We might even have multidimensional realities we're experiencing at the same time. Don't suppress yourself. You can be all you want to be if you just let yourself be. Be outrageous. Let it all hang out. And try to keep a sense of humor about the show. Try not to lose sight of the Big Picture.

When you're in love, you're free to be spontaneous, even off the wall upon occasion. And you can check out any time you want. . . .

Affirmations

1. *I can be myself and be with my lover fully.*

2. *It's safe to be myself in my relationship.*

3. *It's safe to be fully in my relationship.*

4. *It's safe to want to leave.*

5. *I can be crazy and still fun to be with.*

6. *I always have fun being me, so I'm always fun to be with.*

7. *My heart energy is behind all my communications.*

8. *No matter how I act, my partner always gets my love.*

9. *I am always appropriate even when I'm crazy.*

10. *My sense of humor provides relief.*

11. *I always let my partner's love in.*

12. *I know my partner loves me, even when I don't let the love in.*

13. *I always let my partner know I love him/her.*

14. *I am here for my partner.*

15. *I can be here for my partner and myself.*

16. *I never need to separate from love to be myself.*

17. *When I follow my heart, I find love.*

18. *When I follow my heart, I feel more committed.*

19. *I deserve only love.*

20. *My highest desire is harmony.*

—28—

The Honeymoon Ain't Over 'Til the Fat Lady Sings

Every surprise is a lesson in disguise.

George really thought they were over the hump. He honestly felt he could see the light at the end of the tunnel. He truly believed he had finally shaken off his allergy to married life and that there was a chance he might live happily ever after. George's conclusion, however, was a bit premature. The one thing he had failed to take into consideration was that he was in Mexico, where they save the best for last.

They checked out of El Presidente after seven glorious days in heaven. Now they were at the airport, waiting to check out of Mexico. It was Christmas Day and the airport was buzzing. Everyone in the world seemed to be flying home, and they all wanted to leave from this one under-staffed, under-equipped, under-developed terminal. They should have called the place Mañana International.

George was observing the mayhem as Martha was checking them in. Only she wasn't checking them in at all because, as she found out, the flight was full. And it didn't matter that they had confirmed seats or had arrived ninety minutes before departure. So did the thirty other people who had been bumped, all of whom were mulling about, very disgruntled. And by the way, there was no next flight until tomorrow.

In Mexico they should have a saying: if you're early, you're late; if you're late, you're early; and if you're in present time, you're crazy. If they don't have this saying, it is only because its time has not yet come. Because in Mexico there is a very unusual state of mind in which time never does quite get here.

George was thinking all this as the man behind the counter was explaining for the tenth time why Martha and he had been bumped. The man was talking in his very best and most polite broken English, very apologetic but helpless to do anything about the situation. As George observed the man's mouth move, suddenly he didn't hear any words but just was watching the man's lips flapping in the breeze and all he could hear was the sound and the fury of his own heart pounding like a sledgehammer. And the next thing he knew, without knowing how he did it, he had lifted this diminutive Aeromexico employee by the collar about three feet off the ground, half over the counter so that his nose was pressed ever so slightly against George's.

"We would like our seat assignments now, *sí?*" said George calmly, ignoring the Excedrin headache #99 that was splitting his skull in two.

"You must put me down, sir."

"Why?"

"You are strangling me, sir."

"At least we agree on that."

And then the little Mexican put two fingers in his mouth and whistled for the police, who appeared faster than any Aeromexico plane could fly, and who arrested George, handcuffing his hands behind his back and escorting him to the stationhouse, Martha at his side.

George was sitting in a cell so dirty no roach would enter. He was awaiting Mexican justice. The police were going through their bags while Martha protested vigorously. The reason she was so vigorous was the two joints she had hidden in her cosmetics case.

"What is this?" the fat policeman with the mustache asked, sniffing the two joints.

"It's a . . . a cigarette. I always roll my own," Martha tried weakly. George's eyes spun in their sockets as he watched the scene from behind the bars he held.

"Oh, a cigarette!" the mustache said to his tall, lean, droopy-eyed partner.

"Perhaps we should smoke it, no?"

And that's just what they did. And a funny thing happened when

they took a few drags; they got stoned and they laughed and they told
jokes and they talked about their favorite movies. And George thought
he was going out of his mind, watching this Mexican Laurel and Hardy
show. Martha just shrugged her shoulders and shook her head. She
didn't know what was going on.

"Good cigarette," said Droopy-eyes.

"Excellent," confirmed Mustache.

"Very high-quality tobacco."

"Very high."

"Did you see the movie where the Mexicans take over the USA? That
was funny."

"You mean, the one where El Loco marries the Vice President, and
he is a woman and he marries her and kills the President? Ha, ha!"

George suddenly realized that these two comedians were discussing
the movie he had turned down. It had never been released in the States,
God save America, but it had been a sensation in Mexico. He shouted at
Laurel and Hardy, getting their attention, and then told them he was an
American movie star who had almost played El Loco in that movie.

"No shit?" said Droopy-eyes.

"Oh yeah?" said Mustache, suspicious. "If you know this character
so good, prove it."

"But how?"

"Hmm," he said, looking at Droopy-eyes. "He could sing the title
song for us."

"Yes. Sing it for us, señor."

George closed his eyes and, grateful to his photographic memory,
sang for his supper, in a manner of speaking.

> People are saying everywhere I go
> That the future of the world
> Lies hidden in Mexico.
> It's hard to see it the first time you go,
> That the future of the world
> Lies hidden in Mexico.
> I promise it is true, señorita, I know,
> That the future of the world
> Lies hidden in Mexico.
> Maybe it takes a siesta
> Like a sleeping dog in the hot sun;
> Maybe it says mañana

Like a tired worker when the day is done.
But one day I know, as surely as my blood flows,
The future of the world will wake up
And she will be in Mexico.

They applauded. They laughed. And they let him out of the cell to smoke the second "cigarette" with them. And then they recognized George from the movie *El Temple*, where he was a missionary in love with the Indian Princess. And then, since George was now elevated to superstar status, they personally escorted him to the airport where the Aeromexico Flight 62 to Los Angeles still had not departed. Mustache and Droopy-eyes elbowed their way through the crowd, creating an aisle for George and Martha to pass, then escorted them clear onto the plane, where these two Hollywood afficionados bumped two Mexican businessmen out of first class and seated our honeymoon couple. George and Martha thanked them profusely and they all bid each other adieu.

It was on the flight back to L.A. that George made up what he called The Law of Endless Surprises, which goes like this:

When you think nothing else can go wrong,
Something will;
When you think you're over the hump,
You discover another one;
When you think you've found the answer,
You forget the question,
And in the end, for some mysterious reason
Known only to God and Mexicans,
Everything turns out for the best!

WAY #28: THE HONEYMOON AIN'T OVER 'TIL THE FAT LADY SINGS

The lesson of this chapter is that the only thing certain is that there will be another surprise. That life itself is a series of twists designed to shake you out of your expectations and set beliefs. There is, however, the alternative point of view, namely that since there is no fat lady, nor does she sing, the honeymoon never ends. In which case, you might just as well continue having a good time.

Another point seems to be that when you expect the best, the worst happens, and when you expect the worst, the best happens. So perhaps we should all try reverse psychology with life. Except that the worst is not really the worst, only another wonderful surprise in disguise.

Perhaps the ultimate lesson is that the best surprise is no surprise at all. Or else that every moment is a surprise and every surprise a lesson, and every lesson a miracle.

In A Course in Miracles, *it says "There is no order of difficulty in miracles."*

In Mexico, which after all is just a state of mind, they say, or should say, or will say when they're good and ready, "There are more miracles here than anywhere. It's just that they are not in a hurry to reveal themselves."

AFFIRMATIONS

1. *I believe in miracles.*

2. *Every surprise is a good one.*

3. *Things always turn out for the best.*

4. *Whenever I experience the unexpected, I grow.*

5. *I expect the unexpected.*

6. *I'm safe with surprises.*

7. *My future is safe and wonderful.*

8. *The best surprises are the ones I learn the most from.*

9. *I am an optimist by nature.*

10. *I always look for the win.*

11. *There is an abundance of miracles in my life.*

12. *There is a miracle a minute in my life.*

13. *The more things change, the more I learn and grow.*

14. *When nothing changes, that, too, is a wonderful surprise.*

15. *It ain't over till it's over.*

16. *Miracles never end.*

17. *Every moment of my life is a happy ending.*

18. *Every moment of my life is a happy beginning.*

19. *Every moment of my life is the middle of something wonderful.*

20. *The more I'm in present time, the more I'm surrounded by miracles.*

—29—

Give the Little Lady
a Cigar

It was May 1, 1971. Back in L.A. Back home. Back to work.

George was rehearsing for a movie he was really excited about, one he thought would get him an Oscar nomination. The movie was called *Pearl* and was about Pearl Harbor, from the point of view of a transvestite sailor who becomes a hero when he dies saving the life of his drowning buddy. George was getting into character. He had to climb inside this guy's skin to understand the mind and feeling of a transvestite. So he began wearing Martha's clothes when they were home alone together. He cooked. He cleaned. He made the bed and did the laundry. Martha told him he was quite a gal.

She was going the other way. While he was sliding into his feminine side, she was paying the bills, washing the car, watching baseball games, and jogging five miles a day. She joined a health club, got into body-building, developing muscles she never knew she had. After a month she felt incredibly strong, almost invulnerable. She was literally wearing the pants in the family.

One day she and her dad were watching the ball game while George washed the dishes. They were drinking Coors, eating beernuts, and arguing who was better, the Mets or the Dodgers. Alex pulled out his finest Havana and lit up, puffing clouds of smoke into the air.

"Give me one of those," she demanded.

"What?"

"Give me a cigar."

"Cut it out."

"Why?"

"Girls don't smoke these things."

"Well, I want to try one." So he gave her one and she, striking a wooden match across the zipper of her blue jean fly, lit up and puffed away with him. She liked the taste.

She started smoking cigars regularly. George thought it was weird but kept his opinion to himself. Once they went to a Lakers game and she lit up right there in public. Many heads turned to watch the tall, foxy blonde with the big fat cigar. She enjoyed the attention.

George hated the odor of cigars. He lit incense all over the house and, when that didn't do it, he danced around spraying air freshener. The more he sprayed, the more she seemed to smoke. At night he would open the windows wide to let some clean air in, but she would slam them shut.

"I'm cold," she said with finality.

"It stinks in here."

"Too bad."

They were conscious of the new, raw energy between them, but at times it was so powerful it seemed bigger than both of them. One night he served TV dinners—soggy meatloaf, peas, and boiled potatoes. She flew off the handle. She threw the meat, or whatever it was, in his face. He flung his potatoes in hers. She tweaked his nose. He pinched her cheek. Then she jumped him and wrestled him to the floor. She could feel all her newly developed strength and was enjoying the workout. He was trying to get free, but she had him pinned and wouldn't loosen her hold. She laughed.

"Wimp!" she teased him.

"Bitch!" he returned.

The more she taunted him, the more turned on he became. He was thinking, this is against the rules, remembering the fair fighting techniques they had learned in my workshop and practiced so religiously in their relationship. He was remembering the three basic laws: no violence, no cruelty, no destruction! Then he looked up at Martha and saw the taunting glow in her eyes. Fuck the rules, he said to himself. This is the exception, not the rule.

He lifted his legs up in the air and wrapped them around her neck, then rolled his body back and forth, and pulled her up off him and spun free. She jumped to her feet and they confronted each other, face to face, breathing heavily, stalking and clawing at each other like two angry savages. They were both excited, aroused. They could feel the energy like fire between them, like some primordial ritual they were meant to act out.

She pulled off the black silk nightshirt he was wearing. He tore off her khaki work shirt.

"Bitch!" she taunted.

"Bastard!"

She flew at him like a tiger, biting his neck, even drawing some blood. He lifted her up over his head and, like a professional wrestler, spun her around and then threw her down on the bed. Before she could react, he pulled off her Calvin Kleins and thrust into her suddenly.

"Bitch!" she cried and, summoning all her strength, flipped him over so she was on top.

"Bully!" he protested.

"Fuck you!" she said, and that's just what she did.

When it was over, they lay side by side, breathing, shuddering from the waves of energy they both were riding, laughing like on some drug trip.

"Give the little lady a cigar," Martha said. And he reached over for one, lit it, and handed it to her.

WAY #29: GIVE THE LITTLE LADY A CIGAR

Men and women are engaged in an eternal dance, two powerful energy forms in constant juxtaposition, attracting each other with tremendous force, seducing, playing, and sometimes, yes, battling. If you understand the nature of the dance, it's much easier to move with your partner.

Men and women tend to get stuck in traditional roles in relationships. Pictures. This addiction to familiarity can become limiting and stifling in a relationship, especially when each partner is looking to grow into new energy.

Beyond the obvious physiological differences between them, each sex contains elements of the other. There is a common energy to both forms. And that energy is somewhat androgynous, changing from masculine force to feminine strength, from male reason to female intuition, and back again at will. Of course a woman wants to be grounded in her feminine and a man in his masculine, but we are all all things, and when we flow with the changes, we experience a deeper level of the dance.

One of the problems with the feminist movement was that it was based on old forms. Women were seeking power, which was seen as a masculine form of self-expression, so instead of relaxing into a feminine force field, they took on some of the attributes of men. A woman first is a woman and a man a man. To be in balance vis-à-vis sexuality is not to suppress the female to be male, or vice versa. A woman who is comfortable with her male side, and a man who is comfortable with his female side are freer to be more whole with each other. This need not be a battle, or a war. But if one side of you is totally stuffed, it is likely to explode violently at times of increased stress.

So learn the dance. Learn the play. And find the balance within and then express it fully. When love is hot and passionate, it is a fire that is both creative and potentially dangerous. But if you learn to respect and love the fire, you can harness it for the greater good of your relationship.

Affirmations

1. *Thank God I'm a man (or woman).*
2. *I'm comfortable with my male energy.*
3. *I'm comfortable with my female energy.*
4. *I'm comfortable with my partner's male energy.*
5. *I'm comfortable with my partner's female energy.*
6. *I'm safe and powerful as a man (or woman).*
7. *I respect my partner's power.*
8. *My relationship is well-balanced.*
9. *My partner and I are equal.*
10. *I trust my passion.*
11. *I trust my partner's passion.*
12. *I let go of old pictures of how my relationship should look.*
13. *It's safe to be non-traditional.*
14. *It's safe and exciting to experiment.*
15. *My relationship is its own role model.*
16. *My partner and I evolve new ways of relating.*
17. *My relationship is open to new energy.*
18. *My relationship is never the same.*
19. *My relationship is constantly transforming.*
20. *My relationship is a dance, not a battle.*

—30—

The Icing on the Cake

Martha knew she was pregnant. Even before she received the results of the test, she knew it. She knew she had conceived that wild night. She knew it was a boy and that he would be a wild child. Oh how she knew!

After the wild night her body had changed completely. A new wave of feminine feeling took over. She stopped working out, watching baseball, washing cars. She stopped smoking cigars, which to her mind seemed like some weird sign of pregnancy. In retrospect, even the bodybuilding seemed designed to prepare her body physically for childbearing.

Everything seemed perfect to Martha. She felt raw, sweet, tender, vulnerable, primal, and 100% female. At first she had a voracious appetite for honeydew melon and honey-vanilla ice cream. She slept twelve hours a day. Her dreams were peaceful and were about rivers, lakes, brooks, and streams. She woke up each morning intensely happy. She had an image that her relationship was like a delicious chocolate cake and that this baby would be the creamiest, sweetest, richest icing in the world.

She walked in silence on the beach for hours. She looked at the ocean and felt at one with the tide of the universe. Sometimes she walked under the moon, which seemed to stir a subtle energy in her womb. She knew she was pregnant. And the test confirmed it.

George was in Hawaii shooting *Pearl*. He, too, knew she was pregnant before the test came back. He could feel it in his body. He could feel this unborn child pulling Martha inwards, away from him. He could hear it on the phone in the tone of her voice. He could see it in his dreams, which were all about competing with other men for Martha's love—duels, gunfights, fistfights. He'd wake up in the middle of the night feeling furious, jealous, as though Martha were fucking around, which he knew very well she wasn't. She was just pregnant.

Just as her female side had come back, George's male core reared its macho head. His territorial instinct. His possessiveness. His need to conquer and control. His unbridled power. And it was the fact that he brought this new wave of masculine energy, on top of the female he had discovered, to the transvestite role that made his performance so utterly outrageous. George loved playing such a multi-leveled character, but, deep down inside, he couldn't wait to be done filming and back in L.A. with Martha.

When he finally returned, Martha was in a world of her own. She was four months pregnant and showing it. She seemed totally self-absorbed, as though she were in her own womb. He felt shut out, separate, excluded from his own creation. He didn't say anything because he didn't want to upset her. At the same time, he figured out that he had totally recreated his family pattern. Just like his dad, he went off after conception, to Pearl Harbor, to die in a war movie as his dad had died in a real war. George could feel how much he missed his original dad; it just wouldn't go away. And he knew it was a big part of the separation he now felt from his own child.

Finally, he couldn't stand it any longer. He told Martha his gut feeling, that he didn't want a baby if it meant sharing her, that he was both jealous of the baby for stealing her and envious of her for carrying it, that he missed his dad and basically just wanted to be a brat and have a good temper tantrum. He told her he felt like she and the baby were married, and he was the excluded kid. And he couldn't imagine how he'd feel when the kid was actually born, and she'd be holding him, breast-feeding.

His blatant honesty woke Martha up. She realized she had, indeed, pushed him away, emotionally and psychically. She was great. She just got off it and let him back in. She began to share the baby with him.

They'd sing to him in the womb. George whispered sweet nothings through her belly. They made love and told the baby to take cover. One night, after sex, George spread Martha's legs apart, put his mouth to her vagina and spoke directly to the unborn baby as if through a megaphone.

"This is Daddy speaking," he called. "We're getting ready for you out here. We love you, and we're so happy you're here."

Martha could feel the baby kicking in response. George continued, "Don't you worry about a thing, kid. It's a great world out here. Your mom's a knockout and your dad's a maniac, and we're crazy in love, and you are going to be the icing on the cake."

Martha was giggling. George was tickling her, and her body shuddered. Then she was stunned by a voice, a little boy's voice, she thought, and she was sure she heard it cry, "Whoopie!"

Way #30: The Icing on the Cake

Getting pregnant can bring up everything wrong with a relationship. That is why it is so absurd to have a child to save a marriage. The child is just a magnifying glass, enlarging everything between you, positive and negative. He cannot save you from yourselves, but he sure as hell can challenge you.

From the moment of conception, there are three of you. This complicates the dynamics of love enormously, and if you're not conscious you can unquestioningly accept some pretty unpleasant results. You can feel left out as a man while your woman and child bond prenatally. The mother, on the other hand, could unconsciously neglect her husband, as the unborn child draws her attention inward. You can both project all sorts of separation on each other, misinterpreting pregnancy completely.

Both parents can bond with the unborn child during pregnancy and thereby deepen the bond between themselves. No one has to feel excluded. You can both talk and sing to the baby, feel him or her turning, kicking, moving, growing.

When you're unaware, you automatically slip into separation, perhaps duplicating your parents' behavior when they had you. When you're conscious, however, you share the experience honestly and lovingly, growing closer and more intimate. When you're in love with your relationship, a baby is just the icing on the cake.

Affirmations

1. *Our baby brings us closer.*

2. *We can be pregnant and intimate at the same time.*

3. *We can share pregnancy completely.*

4. *It's safe to share honestly during pregnancy.*

5. *Our love is good enough for each other and our child.*

6. *We have enough love to support a whole family.*

7. *Our love is unlimited.*

8. *Our love for each other nurtures our child.*

9. *Our honesty nurtures our child.*

10. *We have a real relationship with our unborn child.*

11. *Our unborn child knows what's going on.*

12. *We can communicate freely to our unborn child.*

13. *We listen to our baby and hear what he or she has to say.*

14. *Pregnancy makes everyone concerned more telepathic.*

15. *Pregnancy nurtures all of us.*

16. *Our baby is a gift from God.*

17. *We are chosen parents.*

18. *We are perfect parents just the way we are.*

19. *We never have to fake it to be good parents.*

20. *Our baby made a great choice.*

—31—

Beauty Is in the "I" of the Beholder

The more pregnant she grew, the more beautiful she became to George.

Sometimes he would just stare at her for hours while she slept or moved around the house naked, as she was wont to do. Martha was a large, busty woman, 5'10", big-boned, long, languorous, silk-skinned, thick flowing blonde hair down her back. And carrying the baby, she took on a warm golden glow and an almost supernatural, larger-than-life appearance. She had what George's acting teachers would have called extremely "high visibility."

He just couldn't take his eyes off her.

"What are you looking at?" she asked once.

"A goddess." She turned towards him, reached her arms around him and kissed him over and over again.

"I love the way I look pregnant," she said.

"You're so vain."

"I think I'll have ten kids just so I can look like this."

George went out and bought himself a Nikon. He became obsessed with photography. In particular, black-and-white shots of Martha. He'd take close-ups, just her belly, her breast, or a portrait of her lying nude on the beach. He looked at her through a thousand different eyes. She began to seem like sculpture, like clay he could shape with his mind into any shape or form.

He built a darkroom in the garage and buried himself for hours, developing. There were days Martha hardly saw him. She began to think he had entered a womb of his own. Then he would appear with the beautiful pictures, and they would stare at them together.

He was fanatical. He hung the pictures all over the walls. He bought dozens of frames, albums, and put the photos in order, giving many of them away to friends, family, and even complete strangers. Once he gave the new mailman a picture. Another time, when a cop stopped him for speeding, he thanked the officer profusely and gave him three spectacular eight-by-ten shots of Martha, the sea goddess, emerging from the ocean.

He couldn't stop himself. He bought a computerized enlarger and kept making the prints bigger and bigger. The house became wall-to-wall Martha. Once he made a print life-size, six feet by three feet. He hung it over their bed.

"If you ever leave me," he said, "I'll marry this picture."

"I could get jealous of myself," she replied.

The coup de grace was a stroke of genius. One day George was driving along Hollywood Boulevard when he got the idea. He made some phone calls, asked Alex and David for their assistance and, even though they thought he was nuts, they went along with the idea. Alex always liked big ideas.

Two weeks later he convinced Martha to go with him to the studio to see a sneak preview of *Pearl*, which was soon to be released. He drove slowly along Hollywood Boulevard, singing at the top of his lungs,

You are so beautiful to me . . .

She noticed it first. She would have screamed, but she was speechless. He pulled the car over, put his arm around her and looked up at the giant billboard he had rented. There was his voluptuous goddess, lying on her back in the sand, her breasts and belly like rolling dunes in the Sahara.

He continued singing,

You ARE SO BEAUTIFUL to me!

WAY #31: BEAUTY IS IN THE "I" OF THE BEHOLDER

What the mind focuses on expands. Your thoughts are creative, and the more energy you add to your beautiful thoughts, the more beautiful life becomes. In short, what you see is what you get.

In relationships, people often forget to focus on what they love about each other. They begin to find fault, looking to criticize instead of ac-knowledge. The judgmental mind casts a shadow over what's really there. You could be with the most beautiful person in the world, but if you lose sight of the beauty, you will project thoughts of imperfection onto your perfect partner. Suddenly, her nose is a bit too long, her breasts too small, and her eyes the wrong color. And the more you see things this way, the longer her nose gets and the smaller her breasts get, until, finally, all you are seeing is a flat-chested Pinocchio with the wrong-colored eyes.

You have a choice. You can perceive your mate through your ego, which is who you are not, or through your "I," which is who you really are. When you are in denial of your true Godself, you see your partner through that denial; whereas, when you are immersed in your own di-vinity, your mate suddenly is your ideal. Your ego says no one is good enough, pretty enough, smart enough. No one is enough!

Your "I" knows better. Beauty is in the "I" of the beholder!

AFFIRMATIONS

1. *I look for beauty everywhere.*

2. *I focus my mind on thoughts of perfection.*

3. *I forgive myself for projecting my ego onto others.*

4. *I now view my partner from my higher self's perspective.*

5. *I acknowledge my partner's beauty.*

6. *I acknowledge my own beauty.*

7. *My partner is a perfect expression of God.*

8. *I can always find something new and beautiful about my partner.*

9. *There is no end to my partner's beauty.*

10. *I see my partner's beauty even when he/she denies it.*

11. *I focus on what I want to see.*

12. *My love opens my eyes to beauty.*

13. *My love is never blind to beauty.*

14. *What I focus on expands.*

15. *I am grateful for my partner's beauty.*

16. *The more I acknowledge my partner, the more I see his/her perfection.*

17. *I forgive myself for judging my partner.*

18. *My partner's beauty increases daily.*

19. *My partner always reflects my mind.*

20. *I dwell in God's beauty and so does my partner.*

—32—

Birth on Earth

Ever since she had dreamed it, Martha had had an ideal birth planned for her child. She read all the books on conscious childbirth and shared them with George. They read Leboyer's *Birth Without Violence* aloud to each other. And they got clear on what they wanted.

It would be underwater, they were clear on that. They really believed that an underwater birth was least traumatic to the baby who, after all, was emerging from a liquid environment in the womb. They found a midwife who shared their ideas and they had a backup obstetrician, in case there was any complication. George focused on the music and the lighting. Martha insisted on the "Hallelujah Chorus," and George felt drawn to Mozart, Vivaldi, and Handel's "Water Music." The clinic they chose was near them in Malibu, and the hot tub was big enough for eight. It would be a perfect birth, the birth of Martha's dreams. And his name would be Oliver, after George's father who died at Pearl Harbor, since they were certain it was a boy.

George spent a good deal of time preparing his son's room. He painted the baby's room blue, hung a blue stained-glass lamp and blue lace curtains, and ordered blue wall-to-wall carpeting. When the room was complete, George and Martha examined it and found it perfect.

Martha's dad, Alex, thought the whole idea was preposterous. He was chain-smoking cigars and not because he was celebrating; he was fuming. He thought George and Martha were off their rockers. He didn't understand this dream birth stuff at all. In his mind, babies were born in hospitals and you decided their sex after the delivery, when you looked between their legs. He had learned his lesson when Martha was born. Why hadn't she? He was making no bets on this one, that was for sure. In fact, he was worried. In fact, for the first time in his life he had what he could only call a premonition, though he couldn't put his finger on just what he anticipated. He kept telling Sarah, his wife, "All bets are off." At first she thought he meant the Mets, but the more he said it, the more she began to worry, too.

Meanwhile, baby was fully conscious in the womb. Baby had enjoyed the nine-month flotation tank almost without exception. Baby loved mother and father, and loved their love for each other almost without exception. Baby felt loved, excited, healthy, strong and welcome to the world, almost without exception. Baby especially loved Alex Kaplan and agreed with his opinion of the birth they had planned. Because the one and only exception to all baby's bliss was the plain and simple fact that he was a she and she was the only one who knew it. No, Oliver would not do at all. Would they change it to Olivier, or Olive, or . . . she couldn't bear the thought of going through a lifetime called Ollie!

So, being of the same strong will as both her parents, she decided not to be born. She folded her arms in the womb, kicked her heels into her mother's ribs, and said to herself, "I'm staying right here!" Martha felt the kick and almost doubled over. She and George were walking on the beach. Baby was a week late already and they were anxious.

"What is it?"

"A kick."

They walked a little further and baby kicked harder. It took Martha's breath away. She sat down on the sand and cried. George sat opposite her and held her hands.

"I think he's angry, George."

"No way. He's just being a boy."

"George, I think he's pissed at us."

"No way."

Alex Kaplan's premonition grew every day. He smoked so many cigars he got sick to his stomach. He called George every night. He couldn't go to work. One night, when baby was three weeks late, he went to a bar and drank too much Jack Daniels. His head was spinning as he wobbled out to his yellow Mercedes 450SL. He drove out on the Santa Monica freeway and saw himself swerving from lane to lane.

It was April 1st, 1972, which should have been a clue to someone, but nobody noticed. George and Martha were spending a quiet evening at home watching "All in the Family." Baby was so claustrophobic she couldn't stand it anymore. She had turned herself completely around so that she'd have to come out backwards, breech like her mom. She still didn't want to come out at all, but she had to do something. So she started kicking up a storm. Like a bucking bronco she kicked and kicked. And she broke the water sac in the process.

Causing Mother to fall down. And the contractions started. George helped Martha to her feet and, gathering the bags they had ready, took them and her out to the Volvo, which he started driving to the new age clinic.

Baby was kicking bad. She was trying to hold on and climb her way back into the womb, but the tidal wave was carrying her down this long, dark chute . . .

"I think he's pissed, George. I really do."

Meanwhile, Alex was swerving real bad on the freeway. He imagined he was on an obstacle course, babies strewn all over the road and he, Mario Andretti, cutting sharply to avoid them. Then he imagined the freeway cracking open, splintering into sections, babies tumbling into crevices, and Alex Kaplan did something he had never done in his life. He screamed. At the top of his lungs he screamed, "No! No! No!" Because the cracks in the freeway were not going away. Because what Alex felt at that moment was the same thing George felt, causing him to make a U-turn, head away from the clinic and towards the hospital. An earthquake! A first class, *numero uno* earthquake. A 5.3 on the Richter scale earthquake!

They made it to the hospital. To the delivery room. To Dr. Evans, the sweet old country obstetrician who was their backup. Who, in the middle of an aftershock, with Martha anesthetized and George bug-eyed, delivered one tough cookie, a breech birth, 11 lbs. 6 oz., bouncing baby girl! When the doctor handed her to George, who held her up in the air, dumbfounded, baby smiled and gave Daddy a great big wink.

George couldn't believe it. He took his daughter to the window where they both saw her at once, the guardian angel smiling on a billboard outside.

The angel winked, too.

Way #32: Birth on Earth

Nowadays it is very much in vogue to plan a perfect birth for our children. We live in the age of Leboyer, Odent, and Verny, the age of prenatal science and psychology. Recent research indicates that the unborn child is far more conscious than previously thought, that this conscious being takes in a wealth of information, makes decisions and forms his, or her, personality largely in reaction to the manner and consciousness surrounding its delivery.

We know, for instance, that a dark, quiet birthing room is less traumatic than an emergency room–type atmosphere. We know not to cut the cord too quickly and to be gentle in touching the newborn. We also know that cesarian, induced, forceps, or anesthetized births, while they may seem like practical choices at the moment, can lead to complications and problems down the road. We know a lot.

In planning your child's birth, it is fine to have a fantasy of the ideal birth we all would love. With birth, as with life, our ideals are the stars we reach for, while, with luck, keeping our feet on the ground. We must all adjust to reality. And despite all our exciting new knowledge about childbirth, there is still much that we don't know. And there are still many unconscious factors that contribute to a birth, not the least of which seems to be the baby's own part in the process, its feelings, thoughts, choices, and karma. The bottom line is still, as it has always been, a mystery, the outcome of which is virtually impossible to predict.

With birth, as with life, technique is secondary, attitude is primary. It is the parents' love that makes the child feel welcome and wanted. No technique can create this love. Nor is there any substitute for it. If there are any physical complications, the baby, more often than not, is resilient enough to recover fairly quickly. The psychological results of birth last the longest. If a mother feels guilty because she thinks she did it wrong, the mother's guilt will affect the child more than the physical trauma. If a father is disappointed by the sex of his child, his disappointment could become part of a permanent personality problem for the child.

The highest ideals of any birth are love and innocence for all parties concerned. It's fine to have your fantasy. It's fine to reach for the stars. But birth on Earth requires that you get your head out of the clouds and keep your feet on the ground.

AFFIRMATIONS

1. I welcome my baby to the world with love in my heart.
2. My baby's birth is the perfect birth.
3. I am innocent no matter how the delivery goes.
4. My child is the right sex.
5. The delivery team is innocent.
6. I forgive myself for any pain at childbirth.
7. I forgive my obstetrician completely.
8. Birth is a miracle no matter how it looks.
9. I let go of my birth fantasies.
10. I give birth the right way.
11. My child's birth is good enough.
12. My baby is happy to be here.
13. My baby recovers quickly.
14. My baby is healthy and strong.
15. My baby is born to be happy and successful.
16. My baby is perfect as is.
17. My baby has everything going for him/her.
18. My baby is blessed.
19. Thank God my baby made it.
20. My baby is not my baby but God's child.

—33—

Who's Keeping Score?

They had been so preoccupied with the birth of their dreams that parenthood itself was a rude awakening. It was as though time itself were a tunnel that ended with the delivery, instead of continuing into a future in which there'd be three instead of two of them. Pregnancy is one thing: having an actual child something else.

When they returned home from the hospital reality set in. The earthquake had turned order and neatness into shambles. Although there was no structural damage, walls needed re-plastering, George's pictures had fallen all over the place, glasses and dishes had toppled and shattered on the floor. It was a mess. Martha was wiped out and fell asleep with the baby in their bedroom. George went to work.

It took him two days to get the place back to normal. Then he re-did baby's room. Blue just would not do. So the drapes went, the carpet went, the blue walls turned pink, and the blue glass lamp became a green and pink one. In 24 hours Oliver's room became Ollie's.

George didn't have time to catch his breath. He drove to the supermarket and bought $200 in groceries. He swept. He vacuumed. He cooked, washed dishes, changed diapers. He did the laundry. And then, when he had completed the whole cycle, he started all over again.

The days rolled by like a fog. Day and night merged into one blur. Martha was so exhausted all she could do was breast-feed the baby and sleep. Only they rarely slept more than three hours at a time because Ollie kept waking up in the night. And she was now the center of their universe. Her needs were paramount.

There were moments of incredible joy, delight, tenderness, and glee when they all played together, making funny faces and sounds, touching and exploring. But mostly, it seemed like hard work, just taking care of whatever needed to be done next.

George did everything. Martha couldn't move. She was depressed. She felt this huge emptiness where the baby had been, and a deep despair gripped her. Sometimes she'd weep for no reason at all, a hollow, aching, bottomless sob that echoed through the house. George would hold her and the baby, who wailed whenever her mother did, and sometimes when she didn't.

When Ollie was three weeks old, George felt like he was three hundred. One day he looked in a mirror and didn't recognize what he saw. He seemed a total wreck, a shadow of his former self, unshaved, unkempt, and ungodly. He wondered how parents had ever survived having children. He couldn't understand how it had gone on for so long without humanity collapsing in exhaustion. He looked at Martha and the baby asleep on the bed, and all he wanted to do was crawl under the sheets with them and close his eyes until it was all over. But he couldn't. He had to go back to the supermarket for more diapers. He was beginning to resent the situation, beginning to feel trapped.

He drove around L.A. for three hours just to be out of the house. When he returned, Martha was hysterical, wanting to know where he'd been and why it took so long. George got defensive and screamed that he deserved a break. Martha was crying again. So was the baby. George was thinking, oh shit, here we go again.

Later that night Martha's parents visited. While the mothers played with Ollie, George and Alex watched the baseball game.

"The Mets stink this year," said Alex, puffing his Havana.

"The whole game stinks," said George, with so much energy that Alex sensed he was referring to the larger game, life.

"You look tired, George."

"I wonder why."

"You're busy, huh?"

"I'm a full-time slave."

"I remember when the girls were born. My whole life stopped. I was nuts. Once I almost left."

"Why didn't you?"

"I was dumb." They laughed.

"Martha's depressed."

"It's normal."

"She doesn't do anything."

"She'll snap out of it."

"I think she blames herself for the birth."

"Of course. She probably thinks she caused the earthquake."

"Probably."

"Relax, son."

"I wish I had the time. There's too much to do. And if I don't do it, it doesn't get done."

"Sounds like you're keeping score."

"I guess I am."

"You can't do that, George. You can't be the scorekeeper and play the game. It's against the rules."

"Who made up the rules?"

"I don't know. God, Casey Stengel, someone up there. Look at it this way, you and Martha, you're a winning team. The champs. So what if she's in a slump right now? So what if you have to carry the load? It's for the team, George. And there's times you can't swing straight and she's there to back you up. No?"

"Yes."

"You gotta be patient, kid. It's a long season."

"I'm so tired."

Alex put his arm around George, who dozed off on his shoulder as the Mets rallied to win with three runs in the ninth.

Way #33: Who's Keeping Score?

It never works to keep score in a relationship. For one thing, keeping score assumes you are opposing teams instead of teammates. It also is a no-win situation. If you measure how much you give vs. how much you get, determining your emotional balance by the difference, you're losing all the time. You are reducing love to a chain of debts, obligations, and responsibilities which can destroy the good faith and trust between you. You become obsessed with either outdoing your partner so he or she owes you one or making sure your partner holds up his or her end. Your relationship becomes a competition instead of a co-op.

When you're in love, you naturally want to give. And when you're giving freely from your heart, you are receiving at the same time. In love there is no border because when you give to your relationship, you give to what nurtures you as well. There may be times when one partner is called on to give more, physically, financially, emotionally, or spiritually. But whatever you give freely comes back to you multiplied. In the long run, when you give, you always win.

If you're in the relationship 'til kingdom come, you tend to have a healthier overview of the whole game. If you're looking for a good excuse to leave, keeping score and feeling ripped off is one of the best.

And sometimes, such as when a baby comes along, it is normal for both partners to feel exhausted, drained. It's nobody's fault. It's just the universe telling you to open up more, take in more love, energy, support. There's more than enough for everyone.

So why keep score?

Affirmations

1. *My partner and I are on the same team.*

2. *I never keep score because I always win.*

3. *I always give freely, not to obligate my partner.*

4. *I love to provide.*

5. *I love to nurture.*

6. *The more I nurture my family, the more nurtured I feel.*

7. *I can give and take at the same time.*

8. *Whatever I give freely comes back to me multiplied.*

9. *I am enough, I do enough, I'm good enough.*

10. *I am appreciated.*

11. *I have unlimited energy at my disposal.*

12. *I deserve to be cared for.*

13. *My partner never resents taking care of me.*

14. *My needs are important.*

15. *I deserve time off.*

16. *I surrender to my partner's support.*

17. *I appreciate all my partner does for me.*

18. *My partner makes my life easier.*

19. *I am never in debt to my partner.*

20. *We are a winning team.*

—34—

Don't Fix What's Not Broken

Suddenly Martha snapped out of her slump. One morning she woke up and the sun was in her eyes and Ollie was giggling and the whole universe seemed to be dancing and singing. She couldn't even remember what had made her so miserable. All at once she was the happiest mother in the world.

She took little Ollie out on the beach, played with her in the sand and the water and showered her baby with hugs and kisses. Life became funny again. She watched George in an apron cooking paella one night and she cracked up. She looked at him washing the car, dusting, ironing, and she thought he was the funniest thing in the world.

"You're a whirling dervish."

"Yeah, I'm the last of the red hot spinners," he said and began to twirl in circles, making Martha and Ollie roll over laughing.

Things started breaking down. The dishwasher went first, then the refrigerator. Then the car. And the TV. He fixed everything. She was amazed by his capacity to repair things and called him her little handyman. He was moving so fast she thought he looked like one of those silent movies all speeded up.

These were the good days, the happy days, the days of blue skies and starry, starry nights. Ollie was such a delightful child. She seemed to be in a constant state of humor, giggling, winking as she had at birth, pointing her finger and biting their noses. Martha and her daughter were inseparable, buddies for life, blissed out on each other.

As suddenly as Martha snapped out of her slump, George fell into a funk. He really flipped out, but nobody, least of all himself, noticed it. His mind just sort of slipped a few grooves, as if he were driving too fast in a lower gear. He was suddenly seeing things differently, altered, and from a very warped point of view.

He was seeing Martha as manic. She seemed happy enough now, sure, but that was just the problem, he thought, she was too happy, just as she had been too depressed before. He was growing paranoid, and she was looking weirder and weirder as a result. He began to see flaws in her where there were none. The truth was, he was mistrusting the perfection that was staring him in the face, projecting his own breakdown on Martha.

She needed help, he decided, so he would help her. He could fix anything, even her. At first he was very subtle. She was tickling Ollie one day, rubbing her nose into the baby's belly and gently twitching her ears. The kid was laughing wildly.

"Maybe she's ticklish," George suggested.

"I hope so."

"Maybe she doesn't like that."

"Look at her. She's having a ball."

He became a worrywart. One morning Martha woke up and sneezed, and he grabbed the baby and wouldn't let her touch her. Another time she was changing Ollie's diaper, and he told her she was doing it wrong.

Martha didn't let it get her down, but she began to notice how off the wall he was. She tried to put it aside until one evening he attacked her for overcooking the linguini. He stomped and screamed that she couldn't do anything right anymore, that all she did was play with the baby, that maybe she should see a shrink.

She was hurt and cried, and he felt guilty. So he did what he always did when he felt guilty, he tried to repair the damage.

"Maybe you need to get out of the house more," he suggested.

"I do?"

"Yes. Maybe you're too isolated from life."

"You and Ollie are my life, George, and I'm loving it."

"Yes, I am too. At least I was. But it's not right, honey. We're just withdrawing into domestic unconsciousness."

"I'm not unconscious. I'm just high."

"I know. I was, too. Until I realized something was wrong."

"What's wrong?"

"I don't know."

"Nothing. Nothing's wrong."

"I don't know."

"I know. Stop trying to fix what's not broken, willya?"

"Everything's broken."

"Not us. Not yet."

And she took Ollie out to the beach where they splashed in the water and played until sunset.

George was meditating, something he hadn't done since Ollie's birth. He was also taking stock of his life. He knew he had it all. He felt close to God, healed with his family, his career was soaring, Martha was everything he had ever dreamed of having in a woman, and then some. And Ollie was the sweetest blessing of all. The more he thought about what he had, the happier he became. He was so happy he couldn't stop crying. And he could see what he had been doing, pushing away all these wonderful things because secretly, in his gut, he didn't believe he deserved to have it so good.

He jumped up and ran out on the beach, looking for her.

"Don't leave me!" he cried to her. "Don't leave me, Ollie!" He held his daughter, hugging her closely.

"Leave you?" said Martha. "Is that what's been going down?"

"Maybe."

"You're such a fool, George," she laughed. "Why would I ever leave you?"

And Ollie winked as if on cue.

WAY #34: DON'T FIX WHAT'S NOT BROKEN

It's almost as though we're allergic to perfection. Whenever it gets too close, we shy away, look for a problem where there is none, and subconsciously try to destroy what we fear we don't deserve.

We're all quite good at making mountains out of molehills. Often we fabricate false issues in a relationship simply so we have something to work on. We're so used to the work ethic, struggling to earn love, that we resist easy love (and easy money) as though they were dirty words, curses. Often, one partner will habitually try to change, improve, or rehabilitate the other, simply to justify the love that's there for the asking.

You can get so addicted to fixing your partner that you push him away from you forever. Or else you could convince him that there is really something wrong and he does, in fact, need repair, in which case he might become dependent on you, and resent you later. Or you could actually fix your partner and then he won't need you anymore, your job will be terminated, and so might your relationship—you are looking for someone new to fix, and your partner is looking for someone who has no need to fix anyone.

If you have a guilt complex, you are, by nature, drawn towards separation, meaning you must keep the good life at an arm's distance, since you do not deserve it. If you know you are innocent and worthy of having it all, you don't have to struggle to justify what God takes delight in you receiving.

You never have to justify love. You never have to work hard at earning it. And you should certainly avoid the temptation to fix what is not broken.

Affirmations

1. *I deserve love.*

2. *My partner deserves love.*

3. *I am innocent.*

4. *My partner is innocent.*

5. *I am addicted to ease, not struggle.*

6. *I deserve to have it easy.*

7. *I deserve perfection.*

8. *My partner is perfect just the way he/she is.*

9. *I choose to see my partner's perfection.*

10. *My partner is good enough for me.*

11. *I am good enough for my partner.*

12. *When I see a fault, I look for a higher thought.*

13. *I forgive myself for disapproving of my partner.*

14. *I love my partner unconditionally.*

15. *I deserve my partner's unconditional love.*

16. *I never push love away.*

17. *I forgive myself for all the times I've pushed love away.*

18. *I trust the reality of perfection.*

19. *I am comfortable with perfection.*

20. *I am relaxed when I have it all.*

—35—

Never Say Never

When George was a kid, he always said "never." His mom would tell him to make his bed. NEVER! His dad would tell him to do his homework. NEVER! His mom, Elizabeth, said he lived in never-never land, and Frank called him the never-never kid.

They had a hard time raising George. But, then again, they had a hard time in general. They argued all the time, or so it seemed. They were always disapproving of each other for one thing or another. Even though they obviously loved each other a lot and, at times, were all lovey-dovey. This was all very confusing to young George, who was a natural ham and learned by imitating.

Whenever Frank had a tough case at the office, he brought his frustration home where he aired it out. One time in particular stood out in George's memory. Frank was tracking a murderer and, apparently, his own life was in danger. (Or so he learned later.) One night he brought his fear home from the office and it turned into ugly rage, and George saw him slap his mother across the face.

"Stop it!" George screamed, and Frank turned on his son.

"Go to your room!"

"Never!"

"Now!" demanded Frank, and George stormed off and locked himself in his bedroom for three days. *Never*, he said to himself, *never* would he grow up like that. *Never* would he treat his children so cruelly. And *never* would he ever raise his hand or his voice like that.

It was November, 1979. George and Martha had moved two years earlier to Manchester, Vermont, yearning for changing seasons and wanting Ollie to grow up in a sane environment, which eliminated L.A. They bought a thirty-acre estate with a big old farmhouse and barn, both of which they renovated to suit their contemporary taste.

Ollie was seven and flourishing. Martha was painting up a storm. She was in her neo-realistic New England period, as she called it, painting huge murals of hunters, farmers, and fishermen at work. She had exhibits throughout the Northeast, from Boston to New York, and was earning in excess of $100,000 per year.

Not that they needed the money. After George won his Academy Award, he became a superstar and had his pick and choice of parts. His standard fee was now one million bucks per film.

Money never spoiled them. In fact, it seemed to free them to live more simply. The more they could afford, the less they seemed to desire. Their days were mostly quiet and holy, and they continued their spiritual practices of yoga and meditation. They also joined a Unity Church, which they attended regularly. They were happy, peaceful, and innocent as ever. Ollie seemed to be a fountain of youth for all of them, and they bathed in her bubbly energy.

They were at the peak of peace with passion and had been together for thirteen years.

He was working on a new film, or getting ready to. It was called *Motherkill* and he played a psychopathic killer who hated his mother and killed pregnant women to spare the children from maternal tyranny. He was, for the first time, playing a villain, and he was drawing on his dark side for material. Martha couldn't understand what drew him to this film, except that it was so well written.

He flew to New York once a week and visited Frank at Red Eye Detective Agency. He was pumping his father for details about the criminal mind. He'd walk the streets of New York with him, and Frank was overflowing with information.

"The thing you gotta get, kid, is that to kill anyone, you have to feel pretty threatened. I mean, the only real motive in a murder is fear. The other stuff is just what you're afraid of. . . . "

"But this guy, he kills pregnant women."

"Kinky, huh? Once I caught this guy who killed ten-year-old boys. It turned out when he was ten, the kids on his block would take turns beating the shit out of him. Now you could say it was revenge. But when I interrogated him, he was still scared of ten-year-olds. In his mind, he was protecting himself, not getting even."

"Weird."

"So maybe your guy is scared of pregnant women, or fat women, or mothers, or birth. Who the hell knows? Of course he's pissed, but underneath, he's fighting to survive."

"Sounds right."

"Is he a vet?"

"Yeah. Vietnam."

"So then he's living in an altered state to begin with."

"Right."

"He's already killed. He knows fear. He knows how to stalk what he fears, how to be single-minded, how to locate and remove the threat. Like a surgeon."

George could feel a coldness grip his soul as he worked on the script on the flight back up to Vermont. When he returned home, he was in a foul mood. Martha could feel the chill as soon as he opened the door, and it wasn't November that blew in, it was George. Ollie went to hug her dad, but he waved her off, like she was in the way.

"Daddy's working," Martha said. She had grown accustomed to George's "leg work," as he called it, those periods of inner rehearsal before starting a movie. At the beginning of their relationship she had found it difficult to adjust to the various characters he brought home. One month it was a priest, the next a war hero, then a transvestite, and then a spy. Sometimes she had not known whether he was really being these characters or just acting. Now she knew there was no difference. He was not the type of actor who could slip in and out of roles in an instant. He had to jump in fully and, once in, it was not that easy to climb out. He just couldn't stay detached.

She respected the way he worked. Sometimes when he was in character, she'd play along with him. They'd improvise scenes which helped him develop his character. But George had never played a psychopathic mother-killer before.

He was very grubby that night. He hadn't shaved or showered in three days. She could smell his kill energy, which smelled like rancid, raw meat. They were sitting at the dinner table, not talking. Ollie was sneaking glances at both of them, waiting for one of them to talk. She had no idea what was going on, but she could feel the tension in the air.

"Can't you shave, Daddy?" she asked, but Daddy said nothing.

"Daddy's working."

"Shut the fuck up!"

"George!"

"Stop telling the kid lies. I'm not working. I'm eating. Jesus Christ!" He flung his plate in the air, which, magically, came down on the table, pork chops and potatoes intact. Ollie laughed at the magic. George swung his arm across the table and this time there was no magic as his plate, beer, and silverware went crashing to the floor. Martha bent over, picked up the mess and automatically took it to the sink.

"What are you doing?"

"What does it look like I'm doing?"

"You're not my mother, goddamnit!"

"Well, we agree on that."

"Don't be sarcastic!" He pushed her away from the sink.

"George, don't!"

"Mother!" he pushed her again. Only this time she pushed him back, hard. He raised his hand to slap her. "I could kill you, bitch!"

Suddenly Ollie, who had seen and heard enough, screamed as loud as a seven-year-old-girl could, *"Stop it!"* George turned on his daughter.

"Go to your room!"

"No. Never."

"Go to your room!"

"Never!"

"Now!"

And Ollie stormed into her room and locked herself in for three days. George turned to Martha, who was shaking her head. He had an overwhelming sense of déjà vu.

WAY #35: NEVER SAY NEVER

What we resist persists. As children, we observe our parents acting like children and decide that when we're adults we'll never act like that. Children often live in never-never land. Then, when we grow up and make the same mistakes, we can't understand why.

It's fine to strive for excellence, to seek perfection, to surpass our parents' limitations. Every generation should take a step, if not a leap, beyond its predecessors. This is a normal progress. Natural evolution. But when you are deeply hurt as a child and say never to that pain repeating itself, you might be both fooling yourself and unconsciously setting up the last thing in the world you desire. The pain you feel as a child is not healed by saying never. It stays in your body. And saying never to that pain might shut the door on that feeling in the moment. But pain will seek a way out, causing you to set up situations which are similar to the past and therefore evoke the same feelings. These are called "past/similars." They feel like déjà vu. Whatever you didn't resolve or understand as a child will repeat itself over and over for the purpose of healing. Especially when you say never.

The more you forgive your parents for the pain of the past, the more you let go of that stubborn resistance called never. You no longer have to resist what no longer hurts or threatens you. You are truly free to be different, without being in opposition to your past. You no longer have to fight, rebel, or prove a point.

Being totally in love with your life, you never have to say never again.

AFFIRMATIONS

1. *I no longer reject my past.*

2. *I am grateful for my past.*

3. *I surrender to the way things were.*

4. *I no longer oppose my past to assert my future.*

5. *I forgive myself for being stubborn.*

6. *I no longer deny my past to affirm my present.*

7. *The more I make my peace with the past, the more I flourish.*

8. *The less I reject my past, the more I flourish.*

9. *I can be different from my parents without rejecting them.*

10. *I no longer focus on what is past.*

11. *I neither focus on nor repress what is gone.*

12. *I'd rather release my pain than cling to my blame.*

13. *I forgive myself for shutting down on myself.*

14. *My parents are and have always been innocent.*

15. *I no longer need to rebel in order to be myself.*

16. *I define myself by aligning with God, not opposing my parents.*

17. *Everyone has the right to be wrong.*

18. *I never have to say never again.*

19. *I no longer persist in my resistance.*

20. *I only persist in pleasure, not in pain.*

—36—

Better to Rake the Leaves Than Leave the Rake

Martha didn't like this movie at all! As far as she was concerned *Mother-kill* was a bomb even before it started shooting, and a dangerous bomb at that. The more she thought about it, the less she understood why George was doing it, what it appealed to in his soul. She finally decided that he had more kill energy in him than she had surmised, and that he obviously had not forgiven his mother for having him before she was ready. This information did nothing to ease her anxiety.

She tried her best to breathe it out, be patient, and trust the future. It was not easy.

He was really immersing himself in the part. He bought himself Army fatigues, combat boots, and an M-16, which he played with around the house. He set up a target on the barnside and practiced shooting for hours. And that was just the beginning.

Martha began raking leaves in self-defense. He had raked the leaves their first two falls in Vermont. This year, he was raking death.

Ollie helped her mom. The two of them raked in silent harmony, stopping and shaking every time the shooting ripped the air. Once Martha started sobbing. Ollie held her and said, "It's okay, Mom. Daddy's at work again."

Maybe all great actors are madmen. Maybe just George. Martha didn't know the answer to this academic question, nor was she much interested in academics. George, no matter how you looked at it, was stretching the limits of artistic freedom when he barged into the fashionable Equinox House one Saturday night, decked in his grubby duds, sporting his (unloaded) M-16, and demanding a Singapore Sling. The bartender, a local lady, served him, then called the State Police, who arrived pronto, and escorted him to the stationhouse for questioning.

George attempted to explain who he was and what he was doing and why. The troopers, two compassionate environmentalists, did their level best to understand. Finally, they called Martha, who came over and explained her husband's behavior, at least to the satisfaction of the Vermont State Police, if not to herself.

The next day she put Ollie on a Bonanza bus to visit George's parents in New York for the holidays. When she returned from the bus station she grabbed a rake and worked with a vengeance. And when George burst into target practice, she burst into tears, her knees shook and she fell to the earth and prayed, "Oh God, let it be over!"

It was November 22, 1979, sixteen years since the assassination of JFK and two days before Thanksgiving. It was the day George took his character to the limits of Vermont's, or any other state's, tolerance. He drove his Suzuki jeep into Manchester, parked on the main street, and climbed up on a roof, midtown, insofar as Manchester had a midtown. He played with his M-16, which was unloaded (score one for sanity), aiming at fat pedestrian women. He jumped from roof to roof, as his character did in the movie, positioning himself for imaginary kills. He focused on several pregnant women who appeared in his sight.

A local farmer was driving his '62 Ford pick-up down Route 7 near the Jellymill. Old Ethan, as they called him, drove this route every day, had for sixty-four years, and today was no different. What was different about today was that Old Ethan just happened to glance up at the roof of his favorite old white Victorian house and noticed a man in Army fatigues, up on the roof, taking aim with a shotgun at Carol Lee Diamond, who was seven months pregnant and the daughter of old Dave Diamond, who owned the Sunoco station in Arlington. Old Ethan had an old shotgun in the back of his pick-up, which he quietly but quickly parked in the Jellymill parking lot. Then he walked across the street and, standing behind a big old maple, took aim at the man on the roof.

Martha was raking the leaves, worrying about George, where he had gone, and wondering if their marriage would survive *Motherkill*. Wondering if she would. She loved him with all her heart. She thought of him as a permanent part of her, but some force seemed to be pulling this permanence apart, like having a limb or internal organ removed. She raked on furiously. She would see it out. This movie would pass, as others had, and George would come home, to her and to himself. Please, God!

George heard the blast and thought he was hit. He rolled off the roof and woke up the next morning in Bennington Hospital with a vicious headache.

Martha was kissing him, and he was remembering the whole sequence of events. He was blushing.

"Oh Jesus," he said.

"You're okay," she assured him.

"Lucky Old Ethan couldn't hit the side of a barn," the doctor added.

"Oh Jesus, forgive me."

"I love you, George."

"Where's Ollie?"

"With your folks."

"Thank God for that."

"I love you, George."

"I love you, Martha."

"Are you okay?"

"Fuck method acting!"

"Yeah."

"Fuck Stanislovski!"

"Yeah."

"Don't leave me, Martha. Please."

"Oh George, don't leave me."

"I did, didn't I?"

"There's fifty ways to go."

"I love you, Martha, and I'll never leave you."

And Martha was thinking, better to rake the leaves than leave the rake!

Way #36: Better to Rake the Leaves Than Leave the Rake

Just how much insanity does one have to endure? The bottom line is: none! You're free to leave any time the going gets too rough. You are never, absolutely never, obligated to stay. And you never have to put up with more than you can, in all honesty, tolerate. After all, your sanity comes first.

If, however, you're in a state of temporary insanity with your mate; if you can see a dim glimmer of light at the end of the tunnel; if you have not lost your sense of humor entirely; if your sense of spiritual wisdom says take a breath, stick it out, rake the leaves, stay . . . if you hear such voices in your mind, you might feel that the end justifies the means, at least in this case, in which case you might as well make the means as pleasant as possible.

Find something simple to focus on. Somethng outside your relationship. Something peaceful to rest on while the roller coaster does its thing. It could be raking the leaves. It could be walking the dog. Or skipping stones. Or jogging. Or doing the wash. Whatever it is, let it be easy and earthy, a place to ground your energy in the center of the cyclone.

Madness is a vortex that tries to suck you in. In any exciting relationship there are periods of questionable sanity. Periods of walking the boundary between reality and illusion. Times when you're crossing a bridge and there's a dark woods on the other side that looks like "the night of the living dead."

You don't have to cross such bridges. You can stay on your side of the boundary. But it is also equally true that you might find it worth your while to go over the edge every once in a while. You might find it a personal growth experience. And while you're going over the edge, your partner can always rake the leaves.

Affirmations

1. *My sanity comes first.*

2. *It's safe for me to go through temporary insanity in order to integrate more love and aliveness in my relationship.*

3. *I respect my limits.*

4. *I honor my spiritual wisdom.*

5. *Whenever I approach a crossing, I trust my intuition to guide me.*

6. *I never trespass on unsafe ground.*

7. *I can ground myself in the midst of madness.*

8. *I am safe with my partner no matter what.*

9. *My partner recovers quickly from any setback.*

10. *I never go too far out of bounds.*

11. *Even when my partner is a little crazy, I am safe.*

12. *My partner respects my limits.*

13. *I know my partner's limits.*

14. *I know my own limits.*

15. *I can stretch into greater safety.*

16. *My patience is a virtue.*

17. *I always have a choice.*

18. *I choose to stay when it serves me.*

19. *It's safe to let my partner stretch me.*

20. *My partner trusts me when I am stretching into greater aliveness.*

— 37 —

Bring Back the Magic

After the incident in Manchester they both went into a prolonged slump. They were like a team without direction, enthusiasm, or motivation. They were playing not to lose instead of to win. They were worse than the original Mets.

Martha had hoped their relationship would rebound after *Motherkill*, which George finished shooting in February of 1980. But it didn't happen. He just withdrew deeper and deeper into a dark cloud, not knowing who he was anymore and feeling like he couldn't be himself in the presence of Martha. He was trapped between a rock and a hard place.

She didn't recognize the man she knew as well as she knew herself. Physically, he was more beautiful than ever, resuming his all-American, athletic appearance. But spiritually he was gray. The silence between them was no longer full of romance and mystery, it was bleak and barren. A wasteland.

Like the Vermont winter. The wind blew bitter and the snow piled up, and the sun, even when it did peek through the clouds, seemed powerless to dent the frigid grip of February.

They lived separate lives, though in one house. Ollie was her usual, bubbly self, but she soon gave up trying to cheer her parents and withdrew into a bubble of her own.

Finally, Martha couldn't take it any more. George seemed to sleep all day every day. All she seemed to do was sweep. Sleep 'n sweep, good morning. She had to do something to crack the darkness, to shatter the

silence. So she did something she had never done before. She wrote a
poem.

> I remember your magic touch.
> I can still feel the places
> It moved in me moving;
> I remember the fire in your fingers,
> Still feel the burning embers'
> Lingering warmth;
> I remember the constant laughter,
> Groucho's cigar and the man
> In a plate of spaghetti . . .
>
> Winter in Vermont is a motherkiller
> And I am another victim;
> Not much to do but huddle by the wood-burning stove,
> Shiver and remember the summers of content . . .
> Oh my long lost lover, I crave your touch again,
> I yearn for the fire and the laughter,
> I shudder for the feel of your fingers . . .
>
> I raise my hands in clenched fists
> That will not give up
> And pray for the power to crack
> This bleak, black, stone-cold silence
> As I thrust them down, karate chop
> And cry, "Bring back the magic!
> Oh God, bring it back!"

   She folded the piece of paper, went upstairs and slid it under George's
sleeping head. He didn't stir. She bent over and kissed him lightly on
the forehead, then went downstairs and sat in the old oak rocker by the
warm stove. She was crying silently, praying for deliverance.
   He was dreaming. In his dream he was asleep and couldn't wake up.
He could see and hear everything, but his body would not respond to his
mind's direction. All his friends and family were in the room, trying to
wake him, but they couldn't. David Levy was telling him about a great
new movie, a remake of *Dr. Jekyll and Mr. Hyde.* Just what I need,
George wanted to say, but his lips would not move. Frank was telling
him about a strange case he had—a baseball player's wife had disap-

peared and nobody knew where. George knew what it was like to disappear.

In his dream he left his body and walked with Hana the Kahuna on a beach in Kauai.

"What's happening to me?" he asked.

"Don't worry. You lost the magic, that's all."

"But where did I lose it, and why?"

"It does not matter. The important thing is to find it and keep it."

She led him along the deserted beach until they came to a cave in the cliffs. They entered. It was pitch black. She took his hand and guided him like a child. They walked deep into the darkness and then sat on a rock. A shaft of moonlight pierced the darkness. They meditated. Finally, Hana reached down and lifted a small flat stone which seemed to glitter.

"Look," she said. He looked, at first seeing nothing but a stone. The more he looked, however, the more he could see. There, on the face of the stone, he saw himself as a child, smiling and beaming in total innocence.

"Put this in your left hand and hold it tight."

"Can I keep it?"

"No. The stone belongs to the cave. But you take the child. If you hold it tight for a few minutes, the child will be impressed on your palm forever." He gripped with all his strength.

The next thing he knew he was back in the room, asleep but not asleep, still in his dream. Alex Kaplan was puffing his Havana, hovering over him.

"The Mets are going to do it this year, George."

Fat chance, George was thinking.

"You've got to wake up, kid."

He really wanted to.

"The magic is back—that's what they're saying at Shea."

And Alex blew a big cloud of smoke into his face, and he suddenly came to, coughing, laughing, and crying.

He was doing the same when he woke up. But when he read Martha's poem, he just cried. And when he ran downstairs and hugged her passionately, they were both crying.

And Ollie got them to go outside and build a huge snow angel by the barn. When they were done, they stood back and admired their creation.

"Look!" Ollie said, pointing to the weathervane on the barn roof.

And they all saw her at once, the guardian angel who threw a snowball down at them. The magic was back!

Way #37: Bring Back the Magic

In any relationship, sometimes the magic is there, sometimes it's not. When it's present, everything flows smoothly. There's an abundance of love, joy, and aliveness, and nothing to worry about. When it's not, you just want to go to sleep and never wake up.

Sometimes, when the magic takes a vacation, you can think it's gone forever. You can feel that the love is dead, the relationship over, and there's nothing to do except leave. And start over again. This hopelessness can seem very real, like a long, dark tunnel without any light at the end.

There are, however, ways to bring the magic back. But first, you must know that you're the magician. Even if you never knew how you made magic in the first place, you were the one who did the tricks, pulled the rabbit out of the hat, made the girl float in midair. You have that power!

Your magic springs from your childlike innocence, a pure faith, a sense of wonder and an open heart. You deserve magic. And when you need it, look to your inner child for guidance. Imagine yourself as the child you once were and shower that divine being with all the love and affection you always wanted.

When you want to break a dry spell, slump, or whatever you call it, it helps to break your routine, do things that are unfamiliar to you. You can write poems, sing songs, or build a snowman. You can read Alice in Wonderland *or go see* The Wizard of Oz *or* Bambi. *You can draw in a coloring book and play with clay. When you break your routine, you create a crack in your universe, and through any crack magic tends to sneak.*

So create a crack, and let the magic come back!

AFFIRMATIONS

1. *I have the power to create magic.*

2. *I am a magician.*

3. *I deserve magic in my life.*

4. *Miracles abound in my life.*

5. *Even when I'm hopeless, I'm still a magician.*

6. *I can bring back the magic.*

7. *Since love is immortal, it never dies.*

8. *When I'm stuck, I relax and love myself.*

9. *I'm safe when I'm stuck.*

10. *I'm never as stuck as I think.*

11. *I'm never stuck forever.*

12. *This too shall pass.*

13. *The best is yet to come.*

14. *I know how to snap out of a slump.*

15. *I am as innocent as a child.*

16. *I am willing to see things differently.*

17. *When I change my routine, I see things differently.*

18. *I always look for the miracle.*

19. *It's safe to change quickly.*

20. *Every instant is a holy instant.*

—38—

Nobody Does It Better

"Look!" he said, handing her the binoculars. She focused in on a couple down on the beach, their private beach. They had bought a villa on the Greek island of Paros in the heart of the Aegean. It was the summer of '81.

The couple was incongruous, a middle-aged American lady, she guessed, and her quintessential Greek boy for a lover. They were naked on the sand, playing unusual sex games. She would crawl across the beach, as if running away from him, and he would crawl after her and mount her, doggy style. Then she'd pull away again and the chase would resume.

"Would you like one?" George asked, sipping some raki, a very potent Greek spirit.

"One what?" she replied, not putting the binoculars down.

"A Greek boy?"

"Oh George, you're so insecure."

"Well, would you?"

"No, George, I wouldn't. I'm satisfied with what I've got."

He pulled the glasses away from her and looked himself.

"Are you sure?"

"Yes." She was kissing the nape of his neck.

"Really?"

"You sure do like to watch."

He put the glasses down and turned to her.

"Up to a point." He took her in his arms and they suddenly couldn't keep their hands off each other, pecking and pawing like two virgins on prom night. This was happening a lot lately. Here he was, forty years old and she thirty-seven, and their sexual appetites were absolutely adolescent. There was no logical explanation. Except that they were two physical animals in the prime of their passion for each other.

It was supposed to be the other way around. After fifteen years of cohabitation, one ordinarily lost some interest. Not George. Not Martha. His touch was more magical than ever, raising goose bumps on her skin and sending tidal waves through every muscle in her body, or so it seemed. She was pure, quivering protoplasm as he unzipped her yellow cotton summer dress and adeptly removed it, leaving her hot naked flesh in his arms. He stood back and looked at her as he took off his shorts. She was a goddess in heat. Her whole body undulated like lava.

"You're too much," he said.

"No, not yet. I want more."

He carried her to the lounge chair on the veranda and, placing her face down, sat on her and gently massaged her back. The sun was setting in the Aegean, and the sky was ablaze, Greek style. They could hear the laughter of the lovers on the beach, and then it merged with their own, and they were consumed by passion, a passion that swelled slowly and steadily, like a huge wave breaking in slow motion, surpassing boundaries they never knew existed.

He was stroking her thighs, rubbing his beard delicately against her bush. She wanted him to come in her mouth, but it was not time to peak. They were still in the foothills.

They made love all night. Just before dawn they went down to the beach, now empty. She lay down on a sensual rock that was sculpted like a Rodin, and played with herself under the full moon, drawing him to her until he entered her cavern and, in rhythm with the sea that gently sprayed them, sprayed her.

They swam until dawn, and then they made love again in the sand, with her on top. When he opened his eyes, the sun was in them, and a brisk Aegean breeze blew his sandy blonde hair.

"You're so beautiful," she said, burying her head in his chest.

"It comes with the territory."

He is one in a million, Martha was thinking, a man for all seasons and reasons. He seemed to know her body inside out, and his familiarity bred neither contempt nor boredom. On the contrary, the more he knew, the more he explored, frequently arousing parts of herself that were so hidden she had never felt them stir before, let alone tingle and burn the way they did now.

She was playing with his nipples without waking him. A song was going through her head.

> Nobody does it better,
> Nobody does it half as good as you,
> Baby, baby, you're the best!

Way #38: Nobody Does It Better

It is one of the great myths pervading relationships, one of the big lies, perverse fables, cruel jokes with a warped punch line. . . . Namely, that passion declines with longevity. That the longer a relationship lasts, the less sexual it becomes. If wines were subject to this myth, we'd miss out on the finest quality of the grape.

Thought is creative, however, and if you blindly accept this myth, your life will become a self-fulfilling prophecy. If you stop and think about it, however, your passion should grow as safety and intimacy increase in your relationship. The more you get to know each other, the more you learn how to stimulate and satisfy yourselves individually and together. And when you realize that the possibilities in sex are unlimited, you know there is no end to the exploration. Most people settle for less in sex, reaching the moon but ruling out the rest of the universe. In a sense we are all beginners as lovers, innocent, sensual beings groping in the dark for pleasure, excitement, and love.

It is important to acknowledge your partner frequently and especially as a lover. We all have our insecurities in this area, and we all need strokes, no pun intended. Moreover, the more you acknowledge your lover, the more love he or she brings to you. You might have a fantasy lover in your mind, a James Bond or Superman, who always does it better than the one you're with. Let go of the fantasy and your partner could become your dream-lover come true. Teach each other to touch each other right. Feel free to communicate, to ask for what you want, to ask your partner what he or she wants. Let go of the defenses that resist feedback in sex, i.e., your partner's suggestions or instructions. Remember, you are responsible for your own sexual pleasure. When two people each please themselves, it's a double turn-on for both.

And, most of all, come from the attitude that nobody does it better. . . .

Affirmations

1. *My partner is a great lover.*

2. *I make great love with my partner.*

3. *Our passion increases the longer we are together.*

4. *Longevity leads to better sex.*

5. *Better sex leads to longevity.*

6. *My partner knows me inside and out.*

7. *The more I reveal myself, the more my partner knows how to please me.*

8. *I know how to please myself with my partner.*

9. *It's safe to be excited.*

10. *It's safe to be out of control.*

11. *It's safe to be touched deeply.*

12. *It's safe to let my passion show.*

13. *My sexuality is innocent.*

14. *I love it when my partner wants me.*

15. *I love to see my partner get aroused.*

16. *I love to be turned on by my partner's excitement.*

17. *My partner gives me new thrills every time.*

18. *My partner has that magic touch.*

19. *My partner is a sexual magnet.*

20. *Nobody does it better than my partner.*

—39—

Midlife Oasis

It was April 1st, 1983, Ollie's eleventh birthday and creeping upon George's forty-second. And the icing on the cake was the two feet of snow that had just surprised Manchester, Vermont.

Somehow snow in April was sweeter than in January, probably because you knew it wouldn't stick around that long. George was watching Ollie and her friends build a huge birthday cake out of snow. Martha was sitting in the rocker, reading the latest script David had sent her husband.

It was like a Norman Rockwell painting, he was thinking, and his mind flashed a series of scenes across his inner screen, stopping at one of an elderly couple, sitting on porch rockers while children played in the snow. He wondered whether such a painting actually existed or he was merely seeing their own future. Pushing forty-two, he had been awaiting a serious midlife crisis to greet him. Which brought his mind back to the screenplay Martha was reading.

He liked the story. He liked it very much, but he felt very exposed in the role he was being asked to play. It was the story of J. D. Dennison, a British lord who gives up his title and property at age eighteen to become a nomad in the Sahara. A kind of Lawrence of Arabia without a war to occupy his wanderlust. J. D. travels with real nomads, lives the gypsy life fully and freely, until one day, when he's forty-five, he stops at an oasis where a beautiful witch seduces him into staying. The film revolved around the eternal inner conflict between the nomadic urge and the nesting instinct. It was called *Oasis* and was a terrific love story.

"How old is this guy?" Martha asked.

"Forty, no, forty-five."

"Is it a true story?"

"I don't know." Martha put the script down and came up behind him, hugging his muscular body as he watched the kids in the snow.

"It scares you, doesn't it?"

"What?"

"Being forty-two. The movie. Aging."

"Yes. It scares me."

"Well, don't worry. We'll never get old."

"Are you sure?"

"So far so good."

He was watching Ollie light the ten-inch candles on her snow cake.

"Ollie keeps me young," he said.

"And when she grows up, we'll have grandchildren to remind us."

They were kissing each other on the couch when all the kids came in and started giggling.

"Can we play spin the bottle, Mom?"

Martha looked up and blushed.

"Only if I can watch," said George, and the kids ran off in hysterics, choosing to watch TV instead.

Later that night George was observing a gray whisker in his beard. He plucked it out, then noticed two more. He looked at the palm of his left hand and saw the inner child Hana had given him, a sweet, innocent golden boy. Was it a choice, he wondered? So far he and Martha had been blessed with healthy, youthful, unaging bodies. People who met them thought they were in their late twenties or early thirties. Could they somehow harness this gift and perpetuate their prime into what most experts considered a period of inevitable decline?

Asleep that night, he became J. D. Dennison in his dream. The nomad. He saw the part fitting him like a glove. There he was, in brilliant technicolor and Dolby sound, crossing the desert on a camel, sand blowing across his face. There he was, an aging gypsy at the oasis, pausing on his eternal journey to water his camel. There he was, meeting the temptress, she seemed to be Martha, seduced into staying. In his dream the oasis was a fountain of youth, bestowed with regenerative powers by the witch. He could see himself grow younger before his eyes, then be torn between the nomadic urge in his blood and his spiritual quest for immortality.

He woke up, and a supreme peace had enveloped him. He didn't remember his dream, but he felt wonderful about his life. He observed Martha asleep and wondered if she would always be as beautiful as she was that moment. Sunlight poured in through the skylight, bathing her naked body in a golden haze. He kissed her gently all over, and she stirred and stretched.

"Good morning, lover," she said, opening her baby blues.

"Don't ever change."

"But George, I always change." She wrapped her arms around him, drawing him to her for another kiss.

"I've decided something," he said.

"What?" She wanted him.

"I'm going to flourish in my forties."

"Of course you are." She rolled over and mounted him.

"And I'm not having no midlife crisis."

"Thank God."

"I've decided to find a midlife oasis instead."

"Oh?"

"My forties shall be a fountain of youth."

"Well, as long as there's plenty of sex."

WAY #39: MIDLIFE OASIS

The fear of aging can drive a wedge between the happiest of couples. Your relationship can seem like a dead-end street from which there is no escape. If you were married 'til death do you part, you might rebel from death through divorce. The feeling of no exit terror that commitment elicits can be magnified ten-thousandfold when seen through the eyes of death.

Many couples go through a midlife crisis when they enter their forties. This can take the form of looking outside the relationship for a younger woman, or man, creating incestuous triangles as an escape. You might also find yourself deeply depressed for no apparent reason, and life could look utterly hopeless. If your parents' death urge is up as you enter your forties, your crisis could be even worse. You might want to quit your job, give up all your responsibilities, and fly off like a free spirit. *You might suddenly revert to adolescent and even childlike be-havior, becoming over-sensitive and over-reactive. You also could be-come obsessed with your body in a negative way, which could throw your sex life into total turmoil.*

Midlife can be an oasis instead of a crisis. By the time you're forty you've experienced enough of yourself and your life to know how to take it easy. You're often beyond basic survival issues which make the early years so anxious. Let's face it, your first thirty years are often about growing up, rebelling, finding yourself, discovering your purpose. Then, during your thirties, you live your life as you choose, plowing full steam ahead, recovering from the confusion of growing up. When you reach forty, you are just about to peak. Your prime is the crest of your life, and if you dwell on the crest, it can last indefinitely. So think of the middle of your life as continuum, not as a precursor to death. Think of your prime as a fountain of youth wherein your mind, body, and spirit are all collaborating to produce ongoing excellence in all areas of your life.

Your relationship is not a deathtrap so much as a lifespring. And the longer it lasts, the more you are replenished at the oasis.

Affirmations

1. My life urge is stronger every day.

2. The longer I live, the more I feel free.

3. I am always young at heart.

4. I am always in the middle of my life.

5. The middle of my life is unending.

6. I am always young in present time.

7. When my heart is open, I am replenished.

8. I renew my life urge daily.

9. My relationship nurtures my life urge.

10. When I surrender to love, I surrender to aliveness.

11. My life is a fountain of youth.

12. The more I relax and enjoy life, the younger I feel and the longer I live.

13. Youthfulness is a choice I make daily.

14. My partner keeps me young.

15. I am always a child in God's mind.

16. My choices never trap me, they free me.

17. The more I celebrate life, the more life I have to celebrate.

18. My sexuality is always young.

19. I always have unlimited energy available to me.

20. I treasure my life too much to measure it.

— 40 —

Dare To Be Different

Oasis was the last movie he made. It was so good, so perfect, he felt complete with acting forever. For a while he didn't tell anyone his decision, not even Martha, but when she told him she felt complete with painting, he understood completely.

When he was forty-seven and she forty-five, they embarked on a new career. They had always liked to sing together, so they became a band and called themselves "Forever." They wrote and rehearsed many songs, and Ollie and her friends became their audience and fan club.

Their friends and family thought they had gone off the deep end. They had to be crazy to quit their brilliant careers in mid-stream, just when they had it made. What everyone failed to see, no fault of their own, was that George and Martha wanted to be together all the time now that there was a rejuvenation going on in each other's presence, and that separate careers no longer served their unified purpose. Besides, they had this genuine desire to create together and the talent to back it up.

David Levy was the first to call.

"Are you absolutely nuts?"

"No," George replied.

"Have you seen a shrink?"

"No."

"Do you know what you're doing?"

"Yes."

David hung up. George laughed, and Martha handed him a glass of champagne, and they toasted themselves. Alex called next, and Martha answered.

"Anything I can do, sweetheart?"

"No, Daddy. We're happy as clams."

"Your mother wants to know if there's anything she can do?"

"No, Daddy. We're really fine."

"Your sister's here. Speak to her."

"Sure."

"Are you absolutely nuts?" Karen asked.

"No."

"Have you seen a shrink?"

"No."

"Do you know what you're doing to Mom?"

"No."

"Speak to your father."

Karen handed the phone to her father as Martha handed hers to George.

"Hello, Alex."

"George. How do you like them Mets?"

"With Gooden on drugs, they've got to be hurting."

"Listen, George, you need some money?"

"Are you kidding? We're loaded."

"Still, you don't want to be stupid."

"No."

"You want to be realistic, George."

"Believe me, Alex, we've thought about this for a long time."

"Maybe not long enough."

"Trust me, Alex."

"Yeah. Kids today are different."

"Kids?"

"I'm not betting on the Mets this year." Alex was changing the subject.

"All bets are off, huh?"

"Yep."

What everyone failed to realize was that they were on the verge of a major breakthrough, and music would be the vehicle. George played the flute like Paul Horn. Martha could belt out a tune like Linda Ronstadt. George sang like John Denver. And Martha played a piano as joyfully as Stevie Wonder. And they both wrote lyrics straight from the heart.

It was the winter of '88. The snow was blowing with a vengeance, and the wind was rattling the windows of an old shed they had converted into a recording studio. They were rehearsing what would become their first gold record. They used a synthesizer, a flute, and a guitar. They sang in perfect harmony.

> *We want to sing together,*
> *I've been singing alone for a long time;*
> *I want to sing in your band*
> *And I want to hear you singing in mine.*
>
> *We want to sing a duet,*
> *I've been singing a torch song forever;*
> *I want to back you up,*
> *Yes, we want to make music together.*
>
> > *Sing together*
> > *Forever;*
> > *Lovers now or never;*
> > *Birds of a feather,*
> > *Fortunate weather,*
> > *Seeking their destiny.*
>
> *We want to sing a new tune,*
> *I've been singing an old song too long;*
> *I want to sing from my heart*
> *And I want to hear you singing along.*
>
> *We want to sing together,*
> *I've been singing solo a long time;*
> *I want to sing in your band*
> *And I'd love for you to sing in mine.*

WAY #40: DARE TO BE DIFFERENT

The secret of staying together is growing together, individually and as a couple. When you stop growing, you lose yourself, and your relationship gets lost as a result. When you're young, it's easy to grow because it's socially acceptable to go through a lot of change, search for values, and seek self-discovery. The older you get, the more you're supposed to settle down, stop changing, and be like everyone else. Normal.

It takes a lot of spiritual courage to stay on the path forever. It requires enormous inner strength to resist the temptation to settle for less than you envision. Dare to be different. Dare to take chances. Dare to take risks and to keep changing. There is no end to change. As you go through life, you have many changes of heart regarding what you want to do, where you want to be, and how you want to express yourself. If you stifle this inherent changeability, you could project it onto your relationship and then want to leave.

Your relationship is never set; it is always continuously transforming. Like love, like life, it is a river you never can hold onto. You can step in it, but it's never the same twice, and neither are you. A good relationship always supports change.

You might want to change careers in mid-stream. Or perhaps move to another country. Or do something you've always wanted to do but never let yourself—climb Mr. Everest, parachute jump, scuba dive, whatever. Do it. Sure, others might think you're nuts, disapprove of you for having the guts to do what they secretly desire. So what? Do it anyway.

Dare to be different!

Affirmations

1. *It's safe to change.*

2. *It's safe to be different.*

3. *It's safe to take risks.*

4. *When I take a chance, I increase my chances.*

5. *I am always growing and changing.*

6. *My partner supports my growth.*

7. *I support my partner's growth.*

8. *The more we grow individually, the more we grow together.*

9. *It's safe to grow apart from time to time.*

10. *Since we're rooted in love, we grow together even when it looks different.*

11. *God supports my growth.*

12. *I have the necessary spiritual courage to grow.*

13. *I'm strong enough to change.*

14. *My intuition guides me through changes.*

15. *I'm free to do what I want.*

16. *I can be grounded and change at the same time.*

17. *I'm on the path forever.*

18. *I love new experiences.*

19. *I never settle for less than my heart's desires.*

20. *I am always different.*

—41—

A Puddle of Fears

When she turned fifty, Martha had her own little crisis. In fact, she was reduced to a puddle of fears. She was still a knockout by any objective standards, didn't look a day over thirty-five. But she felt some major changes moving through her body, not the least of which was she hadn't had her period for three months.

It was August, 1994. Ollie was married, living in Hawaii and working as a midwife in a birthing clinic. George was in L.A., arranging a new album with Columbia Records. Martha was alone at their new home in Bucks County, Pennsylvania, another big old farm they had renovated. She hadn't wanted to move from Vermont in the first place. She had a terrible foreboding about the Delaware River, which bordered their property. But George felt the need for a change, and she did love the horses.

One day she was riding her horse, Darling, a big black mare with a sunny disposition, when she suddenly found her body shaking so badly that she had to stop, dismount, lie down and do some conscious, connected breathing for an hour. She never knew she was so afraid of aging. She thought that was George's territory, and he had crossed it ten years earlier. But as she breathed her fear out of her body, she saw herself as an old hag watching a young George flirt with teenage girls. It drove her crazy. It was embarrassing. And what if it were true, what if she started aging and he didn't? Where would that lead them? God, she didn't want to cross that bridge.

She knew she couldn't discuss any of these feelings with George. He would just tease her, which would only serve to increase her humiliation. This was something she had to face alone. Only she didn't want to face it at all. If only I got my period, she was thinking. If only I could postpone menopause . . . forever. If only. . . .

She was not accustomed to fear. All her life she had had a childlike sense of unlimited safety, unbridled excitement. She didn't know how to handle these rushes of terror that would take her breath away, pound like a sledgehammer in her chest, and leave her feeling totally helpless. Not to mention the hot flashes followed by ice-cold bone-gripping chills.

It was the hottest day of the summer. The sun was pouring through the windows, and Martha was wrapped up in a down comforter, crying on the bed, curled up in a fetal position. She was looking at a photograph on the night table, one that George had taken of her when she was pregnant in L.A. She reached out, grabbed the photo and clutched it to her, sobbing more deeply now.

The next morning she decided she needed someone to talk to. Her dad was in New York on a business trip. Alex Kaplan was eighty-nine but still going strong. She called him at his New York office and asked him to come out that night. He heard the fear in her voice, rented a car, and was in Bucks County by midday. He never refused Martha.

When he saw her, he almost didn't recognize her. She had never looked so ill before, and it worried him, but he didn't let it show. They walked down by the stable to look at the horses. It was hot and muggy, and he was a sweatball. When he put his arm around her, he was surprised by her cold flesh. They didn't talk much, just casual stuff. Later, she fed her dad a fresh green salad from the garden, some cream of mushroom soup and local corn. They drank coffee and watched the Mets beat the Reds. Alex offered her a cigar and she laughed but declined. They went to sleep early.

Martha woke up in the middle of the night and threw up.

The next morning he suggested she go see a doctor.

"I'm so scared, Daddy." She broke down. He held her.

"There's nothing to fear."

"I'm scared of everything. Even the sound of my own voice makes me edgy."

"Relax, baby. This too shall pass."

"I've never been a nervous wreck before."

"You've had your moments."

"Not like this."

"Go to a doctor."

"I haven't been to a doctor since Ollie was born."

"It's time for a checkup."

"I feel like I'm dying, Daddy."

"Don't be stupid."

"I really do."

"Go to the doctor, Martha."

"I guess."

When he left, she called a local hospital, they said to come over, which she did that afternoon. She got a full physical and came home, feeling a little better. She went to the stable, saddled Darling and went out for a ride. Cantering around the ring, she felt free and happy for the first time in weeks. Then, suddenly, she got dizzy, blacked out, and fell off Darling.

She was in a hospital when she came to the next day. George was smiling, and he bent over to kiss her.

"Oh, George."

"Prince Charming is back."

"I love you."

"I love you."

"What's going on?"

"Well, according to Dr. Evans, you are extremely lucky."

"Thank God."

"He says it's a miracle we didn't lose the baby."

"You mean, I'm pregnant?"

WAY #41: A PUDDLE OF FEARS

Don't make an ocean out of a puddle! Fear is not an enemy. It's a sign. Sometimes it's a red light warning you to stop, proceed with caution or not at all. More often, however, it's a green light, signalling more energy, excitement, and pleasure than you're accustomed to. Or a wonderful surprise.

Often you're so frightened you look for security blankets to protect you, be it a person, money, possessions, or a pillow to bury your head in. No amount of security makes you safer. Safety is a result of inner certainty, security a poor substitute.

You're safe with fear. If you know how to interpret the sign, you could even consider it a good friend. Or an invitation to greater aliveness. Or a premonition of something unexpected but pleasurable. Sometimes people feel fear when they are witnessing a natural wonder, such as a volcano erupting, or a childbirth. Whenever you experience overwhelming energy, your mind tends to call it fear. But it might also be a sense of awe gripping you. And awe is not awful, it's wonderful. You might feel a concern for your personal safety watching a big fire burn or a river flood. You might feel little, helpless, and impotent, humbled by the almighty power of the universe. But when you stop and remember that you are not separate from this power, but a part of it, then your fear can rapidly turn to excitement, wonder, and magic.

The fear of fear, anxiety, is more devastating than fear itself. It can paralyze you at the core. Relax. Breathe it out. Remind yourself that you are part of the whole, that energy takes different forms all the time, sometimes stormy, sometimes peaceful. The movement of energy in your body is a reflection of the flow outside. There is a time for every season, inside and out.

Getting comfortable with energy in its myriad shapes and forms is integrating your life urge more fully. And since the ultimate and underlying of all fears is the fear of death, the more you integrate your life urge the safer you become.

In your defenselessness your safety truly lies.

So next time you're reduced to a puddle of fears, remember: it takes a lot of effort to drown in a puddle.

AFFIRMATIONS

1. *I am safe in my body.*

2. *I am safe even when I'm frightened.*

3. *I am no longer threatened.*

4. *I am comfortable with all my feelings.*

5. *It's safe to feel fully and deeply.*

6. *I can now see that nobody's out to get me.*

7. *I am not under attack.*

8. *I am safest when I'm defenseless.*

9. *Since I'm safe, I no longer seek protection.*

10. *My inner safety makes external security superfluous.*

11. *I know how to interpret my fear.*

12. *I can tell a red light fear from a green light one.*

13. *It's safe to be in awe.*

14. *The force of the universe is with me.*

15. *I am open to energy currents in my body.*

16. *Energy is my friend.*

17. *I surrender to energy in my body.*

18. *It's safe to be vulnerable.*

19. *It's safe to be fully alive.*

20. *Whenever I'm overwhelmed, I rise to the occasion.*

—42—

Behold the Little Traveler

It had just thunderstormed, and now it was a bright sunshiny day again. Martha was lying spread-eagle in the warm water, supported by George. Hana the Kahuna was in deep meditation. Two dolphins were dancing in the pool. A double rainbow bridged the sky above.

They were at the Loveborne Birthing Clinic in Kauai. Martha was delivering her second child, Hana was the midwife, and George and Ollie, who worked at the clinic, the support team. The dolphins provided the entertainment, as well as a deep spiritual quality. The feeling in the pool was exquisite. Martha laughed as the dolphins gently nudged her belly, then kissed her head. George had tears streaming down his face, he was so happy.

"Hana?" Martha asked.

"Yes."

"Is there anything I should be doing?"

"No."

"There's nothing much happening."

"Just you wait."

Martha laughed. Hana expounded.

"This child knows how to be born. Your job is just to relax and do nothing."

"Then I'm definitely doing a good job."

They all laughed.

"I see this child is a very old soul."

"How old?"

"Older than you. Ancient. Hmmm. It seems he's coming from another part of the universe."

"He?" said George.

"Or she," winked Hana, the know-it-all.

"An alien?"

"A traveler. I see he is a very powerful being with a very important mission. Hmmm."

"What?"

"I see he has chosen you both to exchange information with."

"What do you mean?" asked Martha.

"Is he an alien spy?" George joked. Just then one of the dolphins brushed against Hana and squealed a shrill song, then splashed off.

"The dolphin says I talk too much. Maybe she is right."

They were silent for the next hour. Martha's contractions were easy but more frequent. She felt no pain in her body, only waves of intoxicating motion. This kid's a real rocker, she thought, then looked up at the mountains around them, waterfalls spilling down everywhere and dozens of smaller rainbows, which the big double one had given way to.

"I must tell you now," Hana finally resumed. "This child is from a planet where all beings are immortal. No one has ever died in its whole history. But it is a very sad place, this planet . . . hmmm . . . they are all alone, separate . . . hmmm . . . yes, that is it, they must be separate to be immortal . . . what a price to pay . . . it is terrible . . . if they love, they would die . . . hmmm. . . ."

"What?" Martha wanted to know.

"This child's parents have sent him to you . . . he will teach you the secrets of immortality in exchange for you teaching him the art of love . . . seems fair to me, no?"

"It's a little high woo," said George.

"High who?"

"High woo. It means far out, flaky."

"Far out, yes. Flaky, no."

"Will he go back when his mission is complete?" asked Martha.

"Hmmm. This I cannot tell, nor would I if I could. You know I cannot read the future, only the past."

The baby crowned at sunset and emerged with the stars. It was so easy. Martha just relaxed her body, released her breath and stretched out like jello in George's arms. She closed her eyes and saw herself sliding down an endless chute, splashing into a pool, and when she opened her eyes, the baby was out. Hana was holding him in the water, cord uncut.

"Behold the little traveler!" she said, handing him to his mother. The dolphins circled them as the baby curled up, face down in the water, Martha supporting him carefully. They all just waited. Nobody said a word. Nobody had a negative thought. Nobody felt anything but bliss. Hana was praying in the silence.

After several minutes, he rolled over, the biggest grin they had ever seen with bright, sparkling eyes to match. He reached his arms up so his hands emerged from the water, stretching towards his father, who moved to hold him between Martha's legs. She stroked the boy's head. Suddenly, he took a deep breath as if coming into his body more. Then he breathed like a little locomotive, placing his hands on his chest, as if fascinated by the movement his lungs created. Hana cut the cord and the baby never knew it. The dolphins were diving in and out of the water, splashing all over the place. The stars were ablaze across the sky and they picked out Orion, for whom they named their boy, having no conscious idea that he had come from just there. It just felt right. Orion. Ollie and Orion, George was thinking. Oh God, what next?

WAY #42: BEHOLD THE LITTLE TRAVELER

Our children have a lot to teach us. That much is obvious. At the very least, they can teach us innocence, playfulness, patience, and practice makes perfect. They teach us about taking care of needs, emotional and physical, about curiosity, freedom, and limits. About being young again. And, of course, they teach us about unconditional love.

But there are other lessons, less obvious and more subtle, which, if we are open to them, our children might teach us. A child enters this life with a wealth of unspoiled wisdom, perhaps gathered from other lifetimes, other planets, or from a direct pipeline to the source of all intelligence. It doesn't matter where it comes from. It doesn't matter that it is not measurable, has no I.Q. It exists and anyone with a brain in his head can see it.

And you can remember all you knew, and perhaps forgot, when you were little, before you were educated into thinking you were stupid and had to learn from your teachers in order to be smart. It is a sad cultural tradition that we deny the natural intelligence of the newborn child. The fact that his body is little and his vocabulary minimal should not mislead you. A huge presence can enter a little form. Perhaps an ancient soul with wonderful gifts to bring. Perhaps a Mozart, Einstein, or Picasso come back to resume his genius. Perhaps an Eleanor Roosevelt, Florence Nightingale, or Sacajawea returning to lead us through a new wilderness.

You don't want to get lost in fantasies about your children, start thinking they're Christ or Moses or Yogananda reincarnated. Maybe they are, but more likely than not it's just your own ego trip. Still, you can let go of your fantasies and still appreciate how fantastic they are. You want to encourage, not squelch, their spirits, listening carefully, and not condescendingly, to what they have to say. Don't dismiss their magical stories as fairy tales. Be open to the altered reality they bring to you. It's just as valid as what you believe is real.

Every newborn child is a high being, uncorrupted by conditioning and brainwashing and socializing and educating. And some especially gifted ones seem to be entering the world as I write. God knows, we need them. And they ask for nothing in return for being here, maybe a warm welcome, a little love, care, attention, no more than we give a car. A little respect.

They are the loveborne, the little travelers, and the gifts they bear may be the very secrets we've been looking for.

Affirmations

1. *I respect my children.*

2. *My children are my equals.*

3. *I let my children teach me.*

4. *I am willing to teach my children everything I know.*

5. *I never teach by disapproving, only by sharing what I value.*

6. *I can be a good parent without being permissive.*

7. *The more honest I am, the better parent I am.*

8. *I listen to my children and they to me.*

9. *When we disagree, I am willing for my children to be right.*

10. *My children are an inspiration.*

11. *My children have an important purpose.*

12. *My children chose me as their perfect parent.*

13. *It's okay to be different from other parents.*

14. *My way of parenting is the right way for me.*

15. *It's okay if my children are different.*

16. *My children see the divinity in their peers.*

17. *My children know that everyone is created equal.*

18. *My children follow their own intuition.*

19. *My children are loving and loved.*

20. *I know I don't own my children; they are their own people.*

— 43 —

What the Dead Said

There was nothing wrong with Alex Kaplan. He was ninety years old and still sailing strong. He smoked his Havanas, worked a thirty-hour week, and walked five miles every day, as he had for the last seventy-five years. He was a physical marvel. In fact, since his grandson Orion had come along, Alex felt younger than he had in years. No, it wasn't his body that got tired. It was his mind. Ninety years seemed like a long time to his limited mind. No one in his family had ever lived past eighty-two, so he was stretching his family tradition and feeling it. He was thinking about his mom and dad more and more, wondering if he would meet them in some sort of heaven. He didn't really think so. His view of an afterlife had changed over the years, and now he saw it as an enormous way station in the sky where he could trade in this life for a better one. A kind of huge cosmic car lot. Alex was looking forward to a newer model of himself.

So one day he decided to die. He slipped into a coma during the night and was taken to a hospital the next morning. The whole family gathered to be with him at his deathbed. George and Martha brought Orion, who was four months old, and very big, almost ready to walk, it seemed. Sally and Beth, Karen and David, Ollie and her husband Jim all arrived. Sarah Kaplan was shaking her head.

"I don't understand it. Maybe it was something in the pizza."

"I don't think so, Mother," Martha said.

"Poor Daddy," Karen cried.

"One thing he's not is poor," Sally commented.

"I don't understand," Sarah went on. "Was it something I said?"

"No, Mom, it's just age."

"What's age? He's only ninety. Strong as an ox. Something is wrong here. Very wrong."

"Relax, Mom. Remember your blood pressure." Sally was trying to help.

Orion apparently found this all very amusing because all he did was giggle and cackle. The more serious they became, the more he roared, which made it difficult for any of them to stay serious very long. Pretty soon they were all laughing and not having the faintest idea why.

David Levy hadn't spoken to George since their phone conversation years before, since George had given up acting. He went up to him now and said, "I was wrong."

"You're right." They laughed and embraced.

"George, I've got a great new script."

"I'll read it."

Martha was talking to her sister.

"What about Mom?"

"She'll probably re-marry and have three more girls," Sally joked.

"She can come live with David and me."

"Or with us," Martha added.

"Not with us. We're not into threesomes."

"I wish you wouldn't joke," Karen was the most emotional.

"Who's joking?"

Sarah started up again.

"It makes no sense. He went to bed all beans. He couldn't keep his hands off me."

"Maybe it was his way of saying goodbye," Sally offered.

"I knew something was wrong when he stopped snoring. He never stops snoring. It woke me up."

"Are you okay, Mom?" Karen asked.

"Of course I'm okay. It's your father who's not okay. I just don't understand. It makes no sense."

Orion burst out in a new round of laughter. They all stopped talking and watched the happy child. It seemed like he wanted to say something to them, but of course he was too young to talk. Or was he? He took a deep breath and let it out slowly, and then, looking at Alex and pointing at him, said, "Gramps!"

Alex snapped out of it all at once. He sat up in his bed and said, "What a waste of time!" Orion roared. They were all stunned by the sudden turn of events.

"Where's my cigar?" Alex demanded, feisty as could be.

"You scared me half to death, Alex," Sarah was crying.

"Don't waste your time, sweetheart. Death, I can now tell you, is highly overrated."

"Do you want some water, Dad?" Karen brought him a glass.

"No. I want a goddamn cigar." Martha found him one, lit it and handed it to him. He puffed the Havana as if it contained immortality, which made Orion giggle.

"Some kid, huh?" Alex said, reaching for his grandson.

"Yes, Dad," said Martha, handing him to her dad.

"Your laughter was a great distraction, son. I mean, death is no laughing matter." Suddenly, he bellowed and so did Orion, and a doctor and nurse came running in, amazed by the scene.

"What a joke!" Alex exclaimed. "There I am in the way station, you know. It was exactly the way I thought it would be. A big, hazy, lazy space with bodies parked all over the place, appearing and disappearing. So I go looking for a famous dead person. You know, someone I can trust. And then I see old Harry Truman, lying there on a cloud, and I knew I had found an honest man. So I go up to him and ask the big question I'm dying to ask. 'So what's the story with death?' I ask him, and he turns his head and looks at me or, shall I say, through me. 'Why do you ask?' he says. 'Well, I'm considering dying and, on the other hand, I don't want to jump in if it's not a good deal.' So old Harry offers me a cigar, we light up, and he gives me the lowdown. 'Don't do it, Alex,' he says. 'It ain't what it's cracked up to be.' Then he explains that when you die, nothing changes. You just stay the same, and your life continues, and even though your body's transparent, and you can materialize and dematerialize at will, everything else about you stays the same. Then he puts his arm around me and asks me how old I am. I tell him. He shakes his head and says, 'You're just a kid, Alex. Don't waste your time dying. It's a bummer.' Can you imagine that?"

Everyone was totally silent. Nobody knew what to say. It was an obvious miracle. Only Alex thought it was normal to die and come back and tell people what the dead said.

And all Orion could do was laugh!

WAY #43: WHAT THE DEAD SAID

One of our favorite ways to leave a relationship is to leave our bodies. We don't have to die to do this, although you always have that option. You can drift off into the ozone, while it's still there, and flirt with other dimensions of existence. You can convince yourself that life outside the body is far easier and superior to life within. You can daydream about being above it all and free of it all. You can dream.

If you are unhappy and don't want to take responsibility for your life, you look for a way out, a great escape, and, if you are spiritual, you look for a spiritual opening—an altered state, a past life, an astral or etheric plane, a new reincarnation. There are no limits to your ability to avoid reality, if that's your objective. The truth, however, is we are who we are and, wherever we go, we take it all with us. Most explanations of other realms make this point very clear—when you leave your body, you carry your karma, like luggage, with you. And whatever is unresolved when you leave is added baggage you carry. All karma is the collection of choices and consequences you have accrued. There is no escape from any choice you freely made. The consequences keep getting forwarded to you.

So, as W. C. Fields said about death, "All things considered, I'd rather be in Philadelphia."

Affirmations

1. *My body is a wonderful place to be.*

2. *I treasure my body.*

3. *I never have to leave my body to grow.*

4. *I'm free to come and go from my body.*

5. *Whenever I get lost, I know my way back.*

6. *I can have it all and my body.*

7. *I am part of the Infinite within my body.*

8. *My body is visible spiritual energy.*

9. *The more I master my body, the more I am a free spirit.*

10. *My spirituality is enhanced by my body.*

11. *I am myself in all realms.*

12. *I take responsibility for all my choices.*

13. *I own the consequences of what I choose.*

14. *My reality is better than my fantasies.*

15. *The life God gives me is the spiritual life.*

16. *I love my life.*

17. *My body lasts as long as I want.*

18. *I never waste my time puttering outside my body.*

19. *I'd rather choose life than death.*

20. *All things considered, I'd rather live forever.*

—44—

Don't Let Them Earth Changes Get You Down

As the twenty-first century approached, the whole world turned super-stitious. And not without reason. Many psychics were now predicting major earth changes with uncanny accuracy. And spiritual leaders were appearing on national TV regularly, urging people to stay calm, get their lives together, meditate, pray, and love each other. The self-improvement business, once ridiculed as just another fad, was now re-garded as a legitimate, viable and valuable form of education, and many of the better universities had spawned Personal Growth Institutes de-signed to improve the quality of their students' lives.

George and Martha became uncle and aunt in 1998. Karen and David had twins, two boys, who were unusual like Orion and, indeed, com-municated psychically with their cousin cross-country. Orion, now four but looking and acting much older, would bring his parents messages from the twins. One day he told them, "The twins say you should write a song about earth changes."

"That's a great idea," Martha said, and George nodded in agreement. In fact, they rarely disagreed with Orion's messages, which were always profound and practical. They had come to regard their son as a special child who, whether he was from another planet or not, obviously pos-sessed a wealth of wisdom which they were meant to know at this point in their lives, and in the life of the planet.

Orion had designed a series of "youthercises" for his parents, a combination of physical, spiritual, and mental practices which took about three hours to do and which they had been doing religiously for nine months now. Their bodies were responding extremely well, Orion told them, and the aging program in their chromosomes had almost been erased. All they knew was that they hadn't felt so alive in years, and when they looked at each other, they still looked as young as the day they had met. So they respected their little traveler, didn't ask questions, and surrendered to the twins with equal trust.

They got to work on their new song. Whenever they wrote, they researched first. In this case, they tapped their computer for all information regarding major geological changes, meteorological shifts, doomsday prophecies, and psychological ramifications of rapid change. They discovered that in the last five years: (1) weather patterns had changed substantially throughout the world—violent storms were more common, extreme heat or cold could now grip any region at random, erosion of coastal areas had accelerated dramatically, and new deserts and rain forests were popping up all over the planet; (2) geological change was also rampant—most of the Earth's major volcanos were now highly active; huge earthquakes were occurring frequently along all the fault lines, and even where there were none; the polar caps were melting down, sending glaciers where they had never been, a new ice age in the making; (3) the psychological damage caused by these rapid changes was phenomenal—spiritual healers reported a 1500% increase in requests over the last two years, worldwide depression was reaching epidemic proportions; alcoholism and drug abuse were soaring, the divorce rate had skyrocketed to an all-time high of 75% of all couples, and suicide was so common, the statistics had become too staggering to report.

It was not the best of times.

On the other hand, good things were happening, too. People who had the courage and vision to change were changing faster than ever. Spiritual communities, alternative economies, and new age cities were springing up everywhere. Millions of people were meditating together daily. And a satellite network for higher consciousness was linking minds and hearts all over the world, enabling the planet's life urge to strengthen even in the midst of all the turbulence.

George and Martha had moved back to Manchester after the great Delaware flood swept away their Bucks County farm. They built a five-thousand-square-foot contemporary masterpiece on top of a small mountain facing Stratton Mountain. It was October, 1998, and extremely hot. The leaves had not turned again. It had been three years since the last foliage season. Now there was just summer and winter, and either season could appear without warning.

They were listening to the new song they had just recorded when it happened.

> *Earth changes! Earth changes!*
> *They're rumbling in the ground;*
> *Earth changes! Earth changes!*
> *Don't let them get you down;*
> *Earth changes! Earth changes!*
> *They're always on my mind;*
> *Earth changes! Earth changes!*
> *Gotta change with these changing times . . .*

Stratton Mountain, which they were gazing at, was an environmentalist's nightmare. Once the glorious crown of Vermont purity, it was now the dark side of the state, crawling with condominiums, developments, shopping malls, and ski resorts. When the big boys had come in with their big bucks, the politicians had sold the mountain down the river. Psychics said Stratton was a sensitive lady, wanting to be left alone. Now she felt raped and her fury was mounting. They said she was a time bomb waiting to go off. You didn't have to be psychic to know they were right.

> *Some people say it's the end of the world,*
> *But I doubt it;*
> *They say we're all doomed and we can't do a damn thing*
> *About it;*
> *When you hear all these things*
> *All these people are saying,*
> *It's tempting to pack up your bags*
> *And head for the hills,*
> *But I suggest praying . . .*

They had never seen a mountain blow up before. But that's just what she did. It started as a rumbling. Windows started rattling and walls started shaking. Then all of a sudden, Stratton Mountain exploded.

In the center of change
There is stillness;
In the center of your mind
There is peace;
In the center of a hurricane
There is an eye;
In the center of your heart
Is release.

They sat speechless and watched the whole thing go down. Orion joined them. It was obvious that the huge power plant had blown up. It was obvious because everyone knew it could not handle the unreasonable demands of the overpopulated, overdeveloped, and overloaded monster the big boys had turned the sensitive lady into. Everyone knew the psychics were right. And as George, Martha and Orion watched the angry mountain burn, it seemed like the end of the world. But it wasn't. They all knew it was just a necessary cleansing, that the planet was being purified for the twenty-first century. They knew they would survive, and that the Earth would be a better place for all the changes.

Earth changes! Earth changes!
They're rumbling in the ground;
Earth changes! Earth changes!
Don't let them get you down;
Earth changes! Earth changes!
They're always on my mind.
Earth changes! Earth changes!
Gotta change with these changing times!

WAY #44: DON'T LET THEM EARTH CHANGES GET YOU DOWN

The planet we occupy is in continuous transformation. It never stops changing. But there are times of greater upheaval, when the changes are more frequent and evident on the surface. These can be times of great personal upheaval as well. When the very earth you walk on is unsteady, your whole life can feel insecure.

These are times to stay calm and release all feelings of urgency. Times to turn inwards, stay centered and grounded in spiritual truth. They may also be times to notice how attached you are to the world around you, be it in the stock market, the weather, or air-conditioning. You don't want your personal state of mind to be dependent on the state of the world mind. You wouldn't want a crack in the Earth's surface to cause a crack in your holy relationship.

Each of us has an unconscious death urge. And the world has a death wish which is the collection of billions of individual minds. Your job is to strengthen your life urge, divorce it from the world mind, and find life-affirming people to support you. You don't want to buy into the prophecies of doom because when the world seems on the brink of destruction to your mind, you are more tempted to give up, chuck it all in and despair. Put your energy on the side of life, which is eternal. Notice the upheaval without interpreting it as doom. The truth is, these are times of tremendous growth and transformation, times of revelation and rebirth. What an exciting time to be alive!

These are also times when each one of us is called upon to get his own life in order, find peace, balance, and personal integrity. And while you are cutting the cords to a constantly changing planet, you and your partner can deepen the immortal bond between you.

These are the days of unlimited opportunity. So don't let them earth changes get you down!

AFFIRMATIONS

1. I remain calm at the center of change.
2. I am safe when the planet is going through change.
3. I change with the planet.
4. I am an optimist; I dismiss all prophecies of doom.
5. I can see the Earth is being purified.
6. My life urge sees me through hard times.
7. My relationship is strong enough to endure the Earth changes.
8. My relationship is strengthened by change.
9. My relationship is in harmony with this living planet.
10. My relationship is balanced, grounded, and resilient.
11. I love this planet.
12. I contribute to the health of the planet.
13. My relationship serves the world.
14. My relationship makes a difference.
15. The more things change, the better they get.
16. My future is safe and wonderful.
17. I stay on the path even when there are temporary obstacles.
18. My relationship is continuously transforming.
19. My partner and I let go easily.
20. The more we let go, the deeper we bond and the stronger our life urge becomes.

— 45 —

It Takes A Lot of Strength To Be Vulnerable

The little traveler had never cried before. Everything else he had learned fast—how to walk, talk, read, write, and even use the computer. He was five years old but seemed to have the body and the mind of a twelve-year-old, at least. Doctors couldn't explain it. George and Martha had given up trying. He was an unusual kid, that's all they would say. And a great teacher. And they were learning so much so fast they rarely even noticed the age of their teacher. It was beginning to seem normal to them that he was their elder.

But his heart was still hiding. If it were true, as Hana had said, that he was here to learn love, then either he was a slow learner or they were doing a poor job. He would never hug them, let alone kiss them good night or anything that mundane. They expressed their love to him frequently, as they did to each other, and although he could not say the words, "I love you" yet, he could feel the warm energy ripple through his body. So he learned his first love lesson, that love was a powerful, nurturing, warm energy that made him feel good inside and seemed to make him grow in ways he never knew he could. This confused him at first beccause he seemed to come into this life with the thought that love was a powerful vacuum that sucked you into itself until you dried up and died. So when they first told him they loved him, he had held his breath and waited for the moment to pass. But gradually he was coming to see that this love was giving, not taking, and that it didn't suck, it vibrated. And soon he was laughing at their expressions of love, as he tended to laugh at most everything, feeling the excitement of their feelings for him. He didn't show it yet, but his heart was beginning to open.

They, on the other hand, were feeling guilty. He was teaching them so much and they felt they had nothing to offer of equal value. If it were true that they were supposed to teach him love, they were perfectly willing. It was just that they had no system, no body of knowledge, no techniques to transmit to him. All they could do was love him. And it didn't feel like enough.

So that when one night he crawled into bed with them, told them he loved them too, and broke down in tears, they both felt a huge wave of relief.

"I love you both so much," Orion repeated over and over.

"We love you, too," George said.

"I do not understand why love makes you cry," the little traveler asked.

"Maybe it just washes away old wounds," Martha suggested.

Orion thought about that for a long time. He thought about his real parents on another planet, how he had never loved them nor they each other, how love was an outlaw, and how now, suddenly, he found himself missing these people he had never felt anything for in the past. He thought about love and immortality, and he could no longer see them as separate. And this was very confusing given his background. One thing he knew for certain was that he had a deep longing to return to his first parents and tell them he loved them. He had always loved them, only now he could feel it safely, and he wanted to tell them that they could all be safe in love forever. But if he went back, he'd have to leave George and Martha, and the thought of doing that sent new rivers of tears down his cheeks.

"I don't want to leave you."

They both looked at each other, George and Martha having no idea what he was talking about.

"Love is so confusing," he said. "Whenever you choose one person to love, you seem to lose another."

"That's a depressing way to look at it," Martha commented.

"It's not that way at all," George said. "You never lose anything of

real value, like love. All you lose are all your little attachments which
get in the way of love."

"I don't understand," Orion replied. "If I left you, wouldn't I lose
you?"

"No, baby," Martha said, hugging him, which he let her do without
any of his former resistance. "You might lose your need to be with us.
But not us. We are with you forever, no matter what."

"No matter where I am?"

"No matter where."

"Oh."

Orion was thinking again. If this was another love lesson, he wanted
to test it out at once. If it were true that physical proximity was not a
prerequisite for love, his logical mind told him that he should be able to
contact his first parents through the power of his love for them. So he
closed his eyes, took a few deep breaths, and directed all his energy towards his heart. At the same time he visualized his parents as he remembered them, two solitary beings, separate but locked into an immortal
contract. He saw them standing side by side under a starlit sky. They
were looking far off into space, it seemed, perhaps wondering where
their son was, what he was doing, even whether he was still alive. Orion
turned up his willpower, and, using all his intergalactic know-how, tried
to make his body appear to them. So he could tell them this one thing
that burned in his heart.

On this distant planet these two immortal beings, who were so alone
together, would have felt cold if they could feel. Would have felt the chill
of love denied between them. But they had never felt love so they could
not feel its absence. They walked out in the desert, where nothing was
growing, nothing had ever grown and, as far as they knew, nothing
would ever grow. The planet was dry. Barren. If they had known more,
they would have appreciated the irony of living forever on a dead planet,
a big, crusty rock rolling like a bowling ball through eternity.

Suddenly, they both had a feeling. There was nothing else to call it.
Even though it was the first time, it was so powerful they could not deny
its tapping at their hearts' doors. And they both saw him at once, their
magnificent little traveler standing in front of them. They were stunned.

"I just want you to know," he said, "that I love you very much. And
that love is wonderful. And it won't kill you. And you should try it
sometime. As long as you have so much free time on your hands."

And then he laughed and vanished into thin air.

When he opened his eyes he found himself weeping in Martha's arms, curled up like a kitten. George brought him a dish of Ben and Jerry's Mint Oreo Cookie ice cream, which Orion was addicted to; he promptly sat up, grabbed and gobbled it down.

"I don't understand this crying business," he finally said. "Does it mean I'm a weak person?"

"No, on the contrary," Martha replied. "It takes a lot of strength to be vulnerable."

WAY #45: IT TAKES A LOT OF STRENGTH TO BE VULNERABLE

The easiest way to leave a relationship is emotionally. You simply deny your feelings, at first not expressing them and soon after not even feeling them, and pretty soon your heart has shut down shop and you are gone. In fact, many people who actually stay together have done just this. They suffer from emotional anesthesia. They're numb. They're absentee landlords of their own bodies. If you're not home for yourself, how can you be there for your partner?

When you surrender to your feelings, they inevitably lead to greater love, trust, and intimacy. And you can feel what you feel, communicate appropriately, take 100% responsibility for the feeling and not dump it on your partner. You can own it and express it for the purpose of releasing it. All your feelings are valid. You don't have to justify them, they just are. They don't mean anything about who you are or who your partner is. You are innocent no matter how you feel.

On the other hand, since you usually have negative thoughts attached to unpleasant feelings, you might want to let go of these thoughts as you feel the feeling. So they don't cause the feeling to come back. So they don't cause you the same pain again in the future. Remember, emotions are healing energy in motion which, when not repressed, lead to greater joy and aliveness.

Often you have judgments on your feelings because you were teased, ridiculed, and humiliated as a child. You were told it's wrong to be sensitive and weak to be emotional. So you grew up all bottled up with unfelt feeling, trying to be tough in order to survive, a rock, an island.

You can continue to sustain such a false reality if you choose. You can, if you're frightened enough, live in a barren world devoid of feeling. But if you want to succeed in a loving relationship, it takes a lot of emotional honesty. And if you want to live in a world where dreams come true, it takes a lot of spiritual courage.

And it takes a lot of strength to be that vulnerable!

Affirmations

1. *All my feelings are valid.*

2. *All my partner's feelings are valid.*

3. *I am innocent no matter how I feel.*

4. *I am innocent no matter how my partner feels.*

5. *My partner is always innocent.*

6. *Since I am innocent, I never have to defend myself.*

7. *All my feelings are safe.*

8. *It's safe to express my feelings.*

9. *I always express my feelings appropriately.*

10. *I take responsibility for what I feel.*

11. *My intention is always to release negative feelings.*

12. *I approve of my emotional life.*

13. *I forgive my parents for disapproving of my feelings.*

14. *I forgive myself for withholding my feelings.*

15. *I support my partner in sharing his/her feelings.*

16. *My children feel emotionally safe in my presence.*

17. *I love myself no matter what I feel.*

18. *I love my partner no matter what he/she feels.*

19. *My relationship is a safe emotional space.*

20. *I am strong enough to be vulnerable.*

— 46 —

The Buck Stops Here

It was Thanksgiving Day, 1999, and they were celebrating their wedding anniversary. As the century drew to a close, they grew even closer, if that were possible. Their latest song, "Turn With The Century," was on top of the charts and they on top of their lives, both personally and professionally. They had shipped Orion off to his grandparents in L.A. so they could be alone for a few days, and were in the middle of love-making when the doorbell rang.

Ollie was five months pregnant and still working at the Loveborne Clinic, which in itself was bringing up a lot of unconscious memories that clouded her impression of reality. Her husband Jim was a profes-sional basketball player, the starting point guard for the new franchise in Honolulu. His career took him away from home a lot, but it had never bothered Ollie until she got pregnant. Now it was bothering her a great deal. She felt totally alone and abandoned, and when she began imag-ining that Jim was about to leave her for another woman, she just couldn't handle it. Jim, for his part, wanted to be close with her when he was home, but she found herself pushing him away, resisting what she thought she most wanted. This, in turn, caused him to spend more and more time away, drinking with his teammates, hanging out in Waikiki instead of catching early flights back to Kauai. But other women were the furthest thing from his mind. He was crazy about Ollie, knew he should be spending more time home, but something was keeping him away and he went with it. In her mind she was losing him, and the more certain she felt of this, the angrier she became. And the strange thing about it was that her anger was not directed towards Jim, but towards her father, George. This made absolutely no sense to her, but that's the way it was.

One night Jim didn't come home at all. He had gotten badly drunk, then sick, so he collapsed at a friend's pad in Honolulu rather than take the last flight home. He thought of calling Ollie, but didn't want to wake her up. He would call first thing in the morning. By morning it was too late. Ollie was on a flight cross country, heading for Vermont.

On the flight to the east coast she went into hyperventilation. She couldn't stop breathing. A stewardess made her exhale into a paper bag, which helped subside the anxiety attack. Or whatever it was. She fell asleep. She didn't remember when she woke up, but she dreamed she was in the womb again, listening to her parents' great plans for their son's future. All the hopelessness, disappointment, guilt, and shame she had for being a woman colored her dream. And worst of all, she felt completely undesirable and unwanted by men. When the plane touched down and she opened her eyes, her first thought was she hated her father. And wanted to kill him. She was at JFK and grabbed a flight to Albany, where she would rent a car and drive to Manchester.

When they heard the doorbell, they tried to ignore it, hoping it would go away. George was in the middle of showing Martha some new sexual move his body could now make, as a result of the youthercises. When the bell kept ringing, they kissed and dressed quickly, and George opened the door. Ollie stood there, glaring at him, looking like the wrath of Khan.

"I hate you!" she exploded and started pounding his chest wildly as Martha closed the door. "I've always hated you! You fucked me up completely. Both of you! Some perfect couple! Perfect fuck-ups!"

Martha didn't know what to say. George thought he should keep his mouth shut. They both wanted to laugh but knew it would be inappropriate, insensitive. Both of them wished Orion were there. To do something clever. Finally, George said, "Is there something we don't know?"

"You don't know anything! Never did! You were so sure I was a boy!"

"That was a long time ago, honey," Martha quoted.

"Yes, we've known for quite some time that you're not a boy."

"I'm not 'not a boy,' goddamnit! I'm a girl. Can't you see what you've done to me?"

"No!" George shouted back, switching to a counter-attack mode. "What I see is you're one helluva woman. About to be one helluva mother. And I like to think that the sins of our birth are not dumped on our parents. So what if we misjudged you before you were born. So what?"

"It was just one of those things, honey. Remember, my dad blew $50,000 betting I would be a boy."

"So pass the buck, huh?"

"No," George said. "Never pass the buck. We made a goddamn dumb mistake. Not to guess you were a boy, but to guess at all. It was none of our business what sex you were."

"We learned a good lesson, honey."

"We thought you had let it go."

"I can't let it go! It's still eating me up. It's why Jim left me. . . ." And her rage turned into deep hurt. She could not speak. Her lips kept moving but there were no words. And then she burst out crying and threw all her vulnerability into her father's arms. George held her, stroking her long, black hair, both of them crying.

"It's not your fault . . . it's mine . . . I know I drove him out."

"What happened?"

"I wouldn't let him touch me. So one night, last night, he didn't come home. So I left this morning."

"Did you leave him a note?"

"Are you kidding?"

"You poor baby," Martha said, then winked at George, who rolled his eyes as mother took daughter into the living room. "You poor unfortunate baby."

George was having real difficulty taking this seriously.

"I'm sorry," Ollie sulked. "I always mess everything up."

"Well, that's all right," George said, sitting in the rocker. "As long as you don't feel sorry for yourself." It was a risk, being facetious at a moment like that. There was a tense silence but then Ollie got it and cracked up. She couldn't stop laughing. There are times when someone says just the right thing to shift your reality entirely, to lift the fog so you can see the light. To wake you up from a bad dream. This was one of those times for Ollie, who finally could laugh at herself.

"You know what I think?" she finally said.

"What?" George asked, starting a fire in the stove.

"The buck stops here!"

"Oh?"

"I own it. I drove him away. I'm that powerful. And that stubborn. And I've clung to being unwanted as a woman. I was so afraid that if I let myself be wanted, I'd disappoint you because you wanted a son."

"We've got one son."

"And how could I ever compete with him? When he was being born, when I was with you delivering him, I was praying he was a girl so you wouldn't love him more than me."

"Ahhh. So you were wrong too." They laughed, then cried some more.

"No. The buck really stops here. No more tears. I drove Jim away. And the good thing is, I know I can bring him back. I've got the power." She winked at her parents, just as she had at her birth. They both recognized it and smiled.

And just then the phone rang and Martha answered it. And it was a sheepish Jim wanting to know if they had heard from Ollie.

WAY #46: THE BUCK STOPS HERE

Science tells us we are the way we are, in part, because of a genetic code our parents pass on to us. Sociology tells us we are shaped by our environment, upbringing, and cultural conditioning. Spiritual psychology teaches us that our thoughts are creative, and our oldest thoughts are the most unconscious ones, yet the very ones that shape our personalities most strongly.

An unconscious thought such as "I'm unwanted" can become a behavior pattern in relationships passed on telepathically from one generation to another, causing repeated rejection, abandonment, and loneliness as surely as a gene can determine the color of your eyes. You can feel as much a victim of these thought patterns as you do of the size of your nose or the shape of your ears. You seem to have no power over any of these circumstances.

Poor you!

The truth is, you have all the power. The same power you used to manifest inherited beliefs can be used to create instant miracles in your life. Once you release the old wounds and the temptation to play the helpless, angry victim. Once you align your power with your highest, most unlimiting, most liberating thoughts. God always says yes to whatever you think. So put yourself in the driver's seat of your own life. You've been the backseat driver long enough. Whatever led you to this moment of truth, you are now free to do anything you want with it. You can trash the garbage, gather the harvest, and plant what you want for the next season. You are the farmer. Not the seed.

So take the big step, the one step from which all others follow. Take full responsibility. You've denied your power long enough. You've generously given it away many times. Enough is enough.

The buck stops here!

Affirmations

1. *I am the master of my own life.*

2. *Since I am in charge here, there's no one to blame.*

3. *My power is sufficient to turn things around.*

4. *I have the power to change my mind and therefore my life.*

5. *I'd rather change my mind than change partners.*

6. *I forgive my parents for their inherited beliefs.*

7. *I can now see my parents' innocence.*

8. *I don't have to believe everyone I love.*

9. *I forgive myself for giving my power away.*

10. *When my results are negative, I change my thoughts.*

11. *My responsibility sets me free.*

12. *My first responsibility is to myself.*

13. *I never have to sell out in order to win love.*

14. *My self-love generates acceptance and approval.*

15. *My partner reflects my higher self.*

16. *I reflect my partner's higher self.*

17. *I can re-create my life the way I want.*

18. *I am as God created me.*

19. *My power is my innocence.*

20. *My innocence is my power.*

—47—

Gratefully Yours

Hana had been planning this New Year's Eve bash for ten years. She wasn't the spontaneous type. And it's not every day you get to celebrate the end of one century and the birth of a new one. So Hana gave it considerable thought, ruminating over details, revising the guest list over and over again, choosing the location with supreme consciousness. She invited twenty-one of her very best friends, some faithful followers, others on a different path leading to the same place. She wanted the whole world represented, so she called to Alaska, Iceland, Ireland, New Zealand, South Africa, China, India, Israel, Greece, Argentina, and Australia to summon the required parties. And she called to Manchester, Vermont, for George and Martha.

Each person received a map which directed them to the appointed place, which was not easy to find, nor did the map necessarily help. You had to have a lot of patience and perseverance to find this spot, which was on the southern side of Haleakala Crater, a newly active volcano, spewing lava to the north. George and Martha trekked in the late afternoon sun, and when they arrived they discovered they were the last ones. They all stood holding hands, all twenty-one of the chosen ones, and watched the last American sunset of the twentieth century.

"It's already the twenty-first century in New Zealand," said the New Zealand lady, who was a famous author who wrote about the Maoris.

Hana asked George and Martha to sing their new song, which they did, everyone joining in.

Turn with the century,
Learn from your memory,
Heal all your history,
Feel all the mystery.

Ring in the new age,
Sing from a new page,
Learn from your memory,
Turn with the century . . .

When there was silence, they all sat in a circle and meditated for one hour. The energy was amazing. Most of these people had never met each other before, yet, after a short time, they seemed like an ancient tribe that always traveled together. Hana opened some Dom Perignon champagne, and they all toasted the new century. Then she said:

"I would like to acknowledge and express our gratitude to the Unihipili of Mother Earth. I would like to thank her for the twentieth century, which to our minds seems like such a long time but is really just a grain of sand in an infinite hour glass. Thank you, our sacred one, for all you have given us these one hundred years, for the earth, the air, the fire and the water, for the birds, the fish, the flowers and the redwood trees. Forgive us for all we have taken without thinking. Forgive us for any harm we have caused anyone or anything, including the smallest particle of dust in the air."

George was looking at her. The light that poured out of her, or was it into her, was a bright white beam shooting through her crown chakra. He couldn't believe his eyes, which were bubbling with tears, so he shut them. Sometimes the best way to watch a miracle is with your eyes closed, he was thinking. Hana continued,

"Forgive all our brothers and sisters all over the planet for their ignorant behavior, for all the wars and thefts, for the rapes and murders, for all the broken promises and unfulfilled promise. Thank you, Mother, for your infinite generosity and patience, and please know that it is with love in our hearts that we ask you to wipe out all our karmic debts as we are born into a new century."

They all sat in silence for a moment, then George and Martha sang their hit, "God Provides."

In my mind God placed a seed,
I have the power to succeed;

In my heart I'm free of greed,
God provides for all I need.
In your hand I place this seed,
You have the power to succeed;
In your heart you know you're free,
God provides for all you need . . .

When they were done, Hana asked each of them to toast the twentieth century. Each time one of them spoke, all twenty-one of them cheered and clanked their champagne glasses, which resonated through the crater.

"I'm grateful," began the New Zealand author, "for the mountains and the music."

"I'm grateful for solar energy."

"I'm grateful for *A Course in Miracles*."

"Well, I thank God for all the children that were born."

"I'm thankful for all the mothers who gave birth."

"I guess what I'm most thankful for is all the rainbows."

"I'm grateful for all my friends."

"I thank God for all the peacemakers."

"I'd have to say it's all my teachers I'm most grateful for."

"I'm thankful for all the people on the path."

"Me, I thank God just for being there."

"And I thank Him for the light."

"I'm grateful for my 1964 Volkswagen bug."

"I'm grateful for my sense of humor."

"I just thank God we've made it."

"I'm thankful for freedom."

"I'm grateful for all the poetry."

"I have to be most grateful for Hana."

"Me, I'm most thankful for Maharishi."

"I'm most grateful for George."

"Martha," said George, completing the circle.

When they were done, they sat in silence for another twenty minutes or so. The stars were brilliant, spread all across the sky, and the volcano seemed to be erupting more, as if sending messages across the galaxy. Hana stood up and led them to a spot several hundred yards to the east, where there was a big pit in the earth. She told them:

"We have been here before. Many times. This is where we have always come to gather, whenever the Earth calls us. Today she has called us all back so that we may bury our karma, so that we may enter the new century free of our burdens. With a clean slate."

Each of them had been instructed to bring at least one item to bury in the crater, to return to the earth, a small symbol of eternal gratitude. Hana started by placing several stones, branches, leaves, and one egg into the hole. Then George placed a bottle of Rolling Rock beer and the screenplay of *Pearl*, his favorite movie. The New Zealand lady buried her Pulitzer Prize. The Irish priest tossed in his rosary. One guy threw in a can of Quaker State Motor Oil. Another added two ears of corn and a gallon of maple syrup. One girl dropped her diamond ring into the pit. Her husband threw his Rolex watch in. Martha placed a beautiful painting of a fisherman in, while an elderly Greek gentleman threw in a bottle of ouzo. When they were all complete, they covered the pit with earth and built a fire on top of their burial ground. Hana concluded the ceremony at midnight.

"Happy new century," she smiled. "We meet again in one hundred years."

WAY #47: GRATEFULLY YOURS

Gratitude is the key to success. It opens the door of everything. Without it you cannot have it all. You can't pick the lock. And the key is yours for the asking.

If you're stuck in the resentment, you won't want to waste your time with gratitude. Maybe when you were a kid, your parents told you you should be more grateful, and you resented their authority, rebelled, and decided never to be grateful for anything. As if the world owed you something. And so you never learned the magical powers gratitude possesses.

If you stop and think about it, it's obvious you have a whole lot to be grateful for, beginning with your life itself, without which you couldn't even complain about what you don't have. You clearly have a host of precious possessions, many of which you would not trade in at any cosmic way station. And in your most intimate relationship there are qualities so priceless you could never put a value on them.

God gives us the gift of life and the gift of freedom to make of it what we will. For this alone, He deserves a little gratitude. He gives us the gift of an infinite universe and a precious planet, full of wonder and grace, on which to construct our lives. If for nothing else, He deserves a pat on the back for the rivers and the oceans, the mountains and the valleys. God gives us the possibility of anything and everything, the opportunity, the chance to take, the leap to make. The Guy In The Sky is surely worthy of a few kind strokes.

The more grateful you are, the more you have to be grateful for. Because gratitude is the key that opens an endless series of magical doors. Sometimes you don't want to be grateful until you've entered the kingdom. But the gates stay locked until you are grateful in advance. In God's mind there is no time. Manifestation is instantaneous. Everything is here now. He has already created everything, and what we call time is simply the measure of how long it takes us to open up to His complete creation.

Whenever you are grateful for what you desire and think you do not have, you realize you already have it, or something better, or that you didn't really want it in the first place.

In your relationship practice daily, weekly, monthly, and yearly gratitude ceremonies. And notice your list of gratitudes grow. Sign all your communications, "Gratefully yours."

Whenever you express gratitude, you release God from the withholding pattern you impose on Him. And to be grateful for every moment of your life is to be a true immortal master.

AFFIRMATIONS

1. *I forgive myself for withholding gratitude.*

2. *I am grateful for my life.*

3. *I thank God for all He gives me.*

4. *I am grateful for all my relationships.*

5. *It's safe to express gratitude.*

6. *My gratitude empowers me.*

7. *My gratitude enriches my life.*

8. *My gratitude makes love last.*

9. *My gratitude adds to my success.*

10. *My gratitude is a gift to the world.*

11. *My gratitude makes a difference.*

12. *I can always find something to be grateful for.*

13. *My partner and I are grateful for our relationship.*

14. *I am humbled by all I have to be grateful for.*

15. *My humility is powerful.*

16. *My humility allows me to witness miracles.*

17. *I'd rather be grateful for all I have than resentful for what I think I lack.*

18. *It's natural for me to be grateful.*

19. *I thank my partner for all he/she gives me.*

20. *I forgive myself for keeping God's love out.*

—48—

It Can Happen to You

She was standing inside her own painting. Not a real painting, but the one she had painted in her mind, so many years ago, when she had envisioned her future, which was now, 2006 A.D.

She stood, arm in arm with George, on the veranda of their beautiful Mediterranean home, on a cliff, overlooking the Aegean, watching the sun go down, a great ball of fire into the great blue Aegean. She was in love as never before. She was a flower in perpetual blossom. No wilting. No waning. Just an everlasting rose. It was a little eerie, she was thinking, that things had turned out so precisely as she had seen them. She wondered if she had time-travelled that day in 1966, or whether her dream had just come true. Or whether it was fate and she had just located hers in advance. It didn't really matter. She was happy. Her children were happy. And their children. And the planet had survived its ordeal, entering a new age of serenity in the first decade of the twenty-first century. It was true that the price tag had been high. Many millions of people had perished in all the upheaval. But she knew they had somehow chosen their own end, and that those who survived were the ones who had chosen a new way of life. A better way. A better world.

They sat down on the western terrace as the sun was completing its magnificent descent. They had been silent for a month now, not from any chosen discipline but from an organic speechlessness which seemed to entwine them more and more these days. Their words were mostly unspoken now. They seemed to have accessed a total telepathy channel between them. A divine sense of communion seemed to bond them as never before.

George closed his eyes and did some conscious breathing as he had been taught years ago. He too was feeling like his dream had come true. He too was remembering the vision he had scribbled on scrap paper forty years ago, amazed at the precision of the way it had manifested. He recalled how his vision had been a blend of the old and the new, as if Cecil B. DeMille and Steven Spielberg had collaborated on it. And that's just the way the world had gone, combining the simplicity of an earlier existence with the best of modern technology. He thought of the way the world had been reconstructed after all the changes, an interlocking network of small cities, no more than 500,000 people in each, local democratic governments electing their representatives to the World Council, which governed the planet according to the New World Constitution, which had been written by a committee of spiritual masters.

He thought of the perfection he and Martha had attained, their hearts attuned to each other and the planet, just like their music. He realized he was sixty-five years old, but didn't look a day over thirty-five. Nor did Martha, whose beauty in the new century was even greater than it had been when they first met. He thought about Orion, who he now believed was a real little traveler, from another planet, who had indeed come to Earth with a special mission and had succeeded. He felt an overwhelming sense of gratitude and well-being, and thought that things could not have turned out better had he himself been in charge. The thought made him smile.

They both felt it at once, a friendly presence in the air. George opened his eyes as a gentle breeze stirred the purple bougainvillea, and both their heads turned simultaneously, as if pulled by one string. The breeze whistled through the flowers as it did every evening when the sun set. Only this night their guardian angel was sitting on an olive tree right in front of them, as two doves circled above. They both shuddered at the memory of their visions and the reality of their perfection. The angel waved at them, winked, and threw gold dust in the air. A golden radiance emanated from the olive tree. It was a moment they would never forget, and indeed had remembered forty years before it happened.

George was contemplating the mystery of it all—the mystery that had first pulled him toward Martha, continued pulling him through each crisis and that still tugged at his soul, steering him towards unknown spaces in her and therefore himself. He used to be terrified of being swallowed up by women, but now that very same energy felt exciting, tantalizing, mesmerizing. He never knew where it would take him, but he had learned from experience to trust, explore, and surrender into it. He knew that Martha was infinite, that the mystery would never be fully revealed, and that the more he immersed himself in the unknown, the more whole he emerged. And that the whole process provoked more questions, new mysteries and unending fascination.

George was headtripping like this, asking himself whether it was the mystery or Martha he had loved all these years. Whether love was just a vehicle to draw him closer to the truth. And whether there was any difference. Or any truth?

Martha was contemplating her dog, Lulu. A border collie with the sweetest disposition this side of heaven, she had died a week before George appeared. Martha hadn't thought of her for years but was remembering how she had added the dog to her vision, and it was the only missing piece. She thought about it and realized that it had been her ego that had tacked the dog onto her vision, that Lulu was the one loss that she had never resolved, the one sore spot in her heart. The one thing she had not let go of. So she took a breath and, with tears in her eyes, said good-bye to Lulu.

She felt George's lips press gently against hers. She opened her eyes and wrapped her arms around him, pulling him on top of her, feeling his familiar weight relax on her. They breathed in unison, their hearts beating like tom-toms. They made love slowly but passionately, like tantric teenagers.

He was lying on his back afterwards, holding her against his chest. He was thinking, is this the end? Is this happily ever after? Now that we have it all, will it all be over?

Martha was thinking, do I really know anything? Who is George? Will we really live forever? Or will we wake up one morning, suddenly old and ready to die, and realize this had all been some wonderful dream, a recurrent dream of perfection, that will never go away but can never be real? Is anything for certain?

They both looked up, suddenly interrupted by two bluebirds making love in mid-flight. They smiled. They watched. They kissed again. And they breathed on and on.

A song was playing in both their minds, which often happened.

A dream can come true,
It can happen to you,
When you're young at heart.

And they both laughed at the silly little melody that each knew the other was thinking. Above them a full moon and distant constellations specked the sky. They could both see Orion. A dog was barking.

Martha suddenly sat up as though being summoned, but all George heard was the dog.

"Look!" she said, breaking the month-long silence. George sat up as the little border collie ran up to Martha, wagging her tail, panting vigorously, then rolling on her back as Martha rubbed her belly.

Lulu had returned.

What next?

Way #48: It Can Happen to You

What does it mean to have a dream come true? As children, we fantasize about many things that never happen. We have many wishes that seem not to be granted. As adults we daydream about a better life, a better world, without ever doing anything about it. Our purpose, in both these cases, is to escape the real world, not change or improve it. Such fantasies never come true because if they did they would be real and no longer fantastic escapes. Reality is opposed to their intention.

But dreams can come true. Some dreams are prophetic—they actually lift you into the future so it becomes now. Other dreams are conscious creations, intentions, goals. Your personal vision may be either of these, and if you hold it to your heart and take the necessary steps, it is inevitable that you end up where you started from, namely in your dream. It starts with you. You must take complete responsibility for manifesting your own vision. You have to be willing to stretch ad infinitum. And you must summon all the spiritual courage required. At times you might want to quit, leave, avoid, and postpone. You can delay your dream if you procrastinate. But if you're willing to learn the lessons instead of running away, you accelerate the manifestation of your vision.

And the process itself may turn out to be more valuable than the results!

You must be willing to surpass yourself. Whenever you surrender to the ultimate stretch, you are rewarded beyond your wildest dreams. You also must be willing to cut cords—energy bonds that keep you stuck in old repetitive patterns. When you break your addictions to the past, you step into your vision of the future.

If you make it happen, it can happen to you!

AFFIRMATIONS

1. *My dreams come true daily.*

2. *The more my vision manifests, the happier the world is.*

3. *The vision is always unfolding.*

4. *I'm always on purpose, patient and persistent.*

5. *I am content with the reality of my vision.*

6. *It's safe to be content.*

7. *My contentment attracts more to be content with.*

8. *It feels perfectly natural for my dreams to come true.*

9. *I ordinarily get what I want.*

10. *The extraordinary is now ordinary for me.*

11. *I never have to leave to attain my vision.*

12. *My vision is accurate.*

13. *My reality is now fantastic.*

14. *My reality is more fantastic than any fantasy.*

15. *It's easy for my dreams to come true.*

16. *I am ordinarily in the middle of miracles.*

17. *There's nothing special about the extraordinary.*

18. *Everything is special and therefore ordinary.*

19. *It pays to pay attention to details.*

20. *My life is a dream come true.*

—49—

Not Having It All

It was 2007 A.D. Summertime. Manchester, Vermont. Orion was home from college. Although he was only twelve, he had completed his senior year at Bennington. Physically, he was fully grown as well, sporting a beard, long hair, but the same old twinkle in his eyes. Clearly, Orion was no ordinary earthling.

Orion watched his parents make music. He knew he would have to leave them soon. His mission was almost complete, and he was preparing to return to his first parents. He had learned the love lessons he had come to gather, and Bennington College offered him no new knowledge, though he had made many wonderful friends. He had decided to leave George and Martha, but not forever. The highest thought he had come to was the result of observing children of divorced parents, watching them alternate weekends from one parent to another. That's what he would do, only on an intergalactic scale, switching sets of parents every few light years. It seemed like a happy marriage of both his worlds. He thought it was funny that divorce had inspired such a happy union, but that's life, he decided.

George and Martha were composing a new song in their studio. They still appeared to be in their prime, and it had become normal to them not to age. In fact it was as if Orion's body had caught up to theirs in physical age, though he still seemed older in spirit. The only times they were embarrassed about their bodies was when a friend or family member commented, like the last time Alex had seen them.

Alex, now pushing 102 himself, had looked at them with a cantankerous expression in his eyes.

"You can't fool me, you know."

"What do you mean, Dad?"

"You know very well what I mean."

"What do you think about the Mets this year?" George tried to change the subject.

"Bah!" Alex waved his Havana. "The Mets are too old. They need some young dudes like you." He laughed.

George looked at Martha who said, "We keep in shape, Dad."

"I bet you do."

"Orion keeps us in shape," George added truthfully.

"That's another thing! That son of yours. He's not a human. He's growing up too fast. You need to get him smoking. Stunt his growth a little."

They laughed at the thought.

"No, I mean it. It's unnatural."

Orion knew that before he left he must leave George and Martha with their final lesson, and that it would not be an easy one. When he looked at their lives, he could feel all their joy, bliss, and contentment. He could see the depth of their love, their enormous energy, and their perfect attunement with the nature of things. These were no small achievements. But there was something they were missing, a dimension of eternity that their vision did not encompass, a dimension without which they would ultimately lose everything.

"Between you and me," Alex had whispered. "I never, in my wildest imagination, dreamed I'd live to be this old. And if I had dreamed it, I would never have imagined I'd feel so great. There's something going on here. You know it, and I know it!"

"The average life expectancy is up to ninety-five, you know."

"There's more to it than that, George. Life extension is one thing. A new fad, that's all. But immortality?"

"We have strong genes."

"Come on, Martha," her dad winked.

"Well, what do you think it is?" asked George.

"Sex. It's sex. We can't get enough of it. And we love it too much to die." He cracked up, and so did George and Martha, who were relieved to be off the hook.

Orion waited patiently for his parents to finish recording. Then he spoke to them.

"Soon I must leave," he started, and George and Martha instinctively held hands. "Do not ask me where I am going. You must understand that I cannot ever leave you. I love you too much to leave."

Orion did not expect the tears that trickled down his face. And when Martha's maternal urge caused her to reach for him, he said, "No, Mom, please. I must continue. There is something I have to tell you before I go. And it is very important that you listen." They sat down on the Persian rug in a circle, as they had many times before, whenever Orion was instructing them. All three held hands, breathed together and felt the energy among them.

"The last secret I must tell you is the piece that will make the puzzle complete." Orion hesitated and George noticed.

"We can handle it, son."

"Yes, you can. You have handled so much."

"What is it?" Martha wanted to know.

"Not having it all."

"What?"

"The final secret is *not* having it *all*. You must always walk the fine line between having it all and not having it all, between certainty and uncertainty, between faith and doubt, and even between life and death. You must never veer too far to one side or, if you do, correct your course immediately. And even each other! You must always have and not have each other. You must stay and you must leave, and you must do neither. You must walk that fine thin line in between. Right on the border. The tightrope."

There was nothing they could say. They understood, and they didn't understand. They wanted to ask what he meant, but they had no questions. And then, all at once, when he knew they had received the lesson, Orion vanished into thin air.

WAY #49: NOT HAVING IT ALL

Often we measure our success by how much we have. Do we have a house, a car, a good job, a lot of money? Do we have a good loving relationship? Do we have God? But the more subtle measure of success is in not *having what we have.*

In a sense you can never have a relationship. You are in *a relationship, in love, but it is not something you can own, possess, contain. The very idea that you can have it limits it from being all it can be. The same is true with all your material possessions. You have them, but you don't. They are just passing through your hands. Money, for example, only has value in circulation, so, in a way, when you have it, it is less valuable than when you give it to someone else, exchanging it for another temporary possession. Or when you buy property. Do you really own it? Or does the land belong to the trees and the grass, the birds and the bees, the squirrels and the chipmunks? How can you own land? You can live on it, use it, manage it, but in the final analysis it remains God's territory.*

On the other hand, you can get stuck in detachment. You might be so wary of your possessive instincts that you overcompensate and become invested in not having things, be they material goods or an intimate relationship. You could even be in a relationship and obsessively detached. Obviously, if you are compulsive about keeping your distance, you will create sizable separation in your life.

So the trick is to walk the fine line between having and not having. To remember that once you think you have it all, you limit life in a mental container. And life itself is unlimited. And when you're convinced you have nothing, you generate false separation. Remember your magnitude with humility.

Whenever you think you have it all, you don't. And when you think you don't, you do.

AFFIRMATIONS

1. *There are no limits in my life.*

2. *I forgive myself for my possessiveness.*

3. *The less I possess, the more I have.*

4. *I measure my success in quality, not quantity.*

5. *I never take life for granted.*

6. *I never take my relationship for granted.*

7. *I'd rather be in love than possess a lover.*

8. *God owns everything I have.*

9. *I thank God for letting me play with His possessions.*

10. *I am always open to more.*

11. *It's safe to be involved.*

12. *I never have to detach to love.*

13. *I love being involved.*

14. *I can be involved and not possessive.*

15. *I can be intimate and not territorial.*

16. *My life unfolds in God's territory.*

17. *I count my blessings, not my possessions.*

18. *My connection with the infinite is more important than having it all.*

19. *Thank God I have nothing.*

20. *Thank God I have everything.*

—50—

Breaking Up Is
Hard To Do

Although their little traveler had vanished, they still felt his presence. And they gave considerable thought to the meaning of not having it all. On the surface they were happy as could be and enjoyed a wonderful winter of cross-country skiing, composing and recording new songs. And when spring came, they planted their most ambitious garden to date. George was so pleased with his little seedlings he couldn't contain his joy. But then he began to wonder if he was too attached, so he became sullen, downplaying his pleasure. Then he began downplaying his whole life.

He didn't say a word to Martha, but something was brewing inside him, and he had no idea where it would lead him. In fact, he had no idea at any given moment what he would do the next. One morning he woke up with the impulse to drive to Boston. So he did. When he got there, he couldn't figure out what he was doing there. So he ate two dozen Wellfleet oysters and drove home. Another day he felt an overwhelming desire to see a Mets game at Shea Stadium. So he drove to New York, went to the game and then left in the seventh inning even though a forty-two-year-old Dwight Gooden was pitching a no-hitter.

Martha said nothing about George's erratic behavior. In fact, she hardly seemed to notice it. She was withdrawing more and more into herself, spending endless hours in deep meditation, seeking her own sense of direction. The more George took off, the more she was still.

So when George decided to leave her, he didn't know how to tell her. For one thing, he had no reason in the world to go. Their life was perfect. She was perfect. He could not have asked for more. And if he had wanted more, he would have asked, and she would have given. Was he overcompensating for having it all? Was he stuck in detachment? He didn't think so. He just knew it was time to move on.

For a week he rehearsed breaking the news to her. He paced around the house talking to himself, trying to make sense of nonsense and logic of intuition. He slammed doors in frustration. He even smoked cigarettes, trying to get her attention, and when that didn't work, he packed his suitcase and then unpacked it, then packed it again. Still, she didn't seem to notice or care.

It was when he finally gave up and decided he could not leave, it was too crazy, he couldn't do that to her, that she came to him and said, "George, I'm leaving."

And so they split up. After forty-one years of learning how to stay, they put their house on the market, made all the necessary financial arrangements to separate, and by July 1st, each of them was fully prepared. There was no fanfare about leaving, no tears, no regrets, no sweet sorrow. They were leaving each other totally fulfilled, a permanent part of each other, with nothing but joy in their hearts. They hugged tenderly, kissed once, didn't say a word, and drove off in opposite directions.

It's funny, George was thinking, how you think your life is going one way, how all the steps you've taken seem to be leading to a certain destination and then, when you arrive, it's not the way you thought it would be at all, and everything looks totally unfamiliar, like a dreamscape. That's how he felt, like he was driving through a dream, and it didn't matter where he turned because any scene, any place could appear any time. He was driving an old blue BMW. He drove day and night for three days, too wired to sleep, and when he finally pulled the car over and got out, he found himself on a mesa in eastern Arizona, in a town called Oraibi. He was on the Hopi Indian reservation.

Martha was on an unusual pilgrimage and she knew it. She was a seeker in search of nothing in particular, in quest of a question more than an answer. She drove the new Volvo aimlessly and found herself at the Burlington airport. She parked in long-term parking, strapped on her backpack, walked into the departure terminal, and examined the big board to see what flights were going where.

When she landed in San Francisco, she rented a Buick and drove south. She reached Big Sur four hours later, then turned east and drove up into the mountains. When she arrived at Tassajara, at the Zen monastery, the big Tibetan bells were all ringing. She smiled as she got out of her car. She took a few deep breaths and closed her eyes, letting the sound of the bells move her. She felt like she had come home.

George stayed with the Hopi for three weeks. He found the people incredibly sweet, wise, mystical, and powerful. They reminded him of Hana the Kahuna in their kindness, simplicity, and sense of wonder. They introduced him to ancient ceremonies in their kivas, their temples dug into the earth. He found it interesting that Hopi temples went underground, the holiest spot being the deepest, as opposed to all those Western cathedrals that aspire towards a God in heaven. Different strokes for different folks, he thought.

In the kivas he chanted and prayed and danced with the tribal elders. And pretty soon his kopavi, the door at the top of his head, swung open, and a Pandora's box of unconscious imagery poured through. He saw Martha as a Greek goddess bathed in amber light, and he as her devoted priest, protecting her temple and interpreting her oracle. He saw himself as a caveman and she as his son, and they hunted and fished together. He saw Orion as his father going off to war, coming face to face with his enemy, and he was the enemy. He saw Orion kill him with a laser gun.

George grew restless and left the reservation. He drove into northern New Mexico, near the Colorado border, and he gravitated into the mountains where he found a spot that seemed right. He parked the car and walked up into the rocks, where he found a cave he liked. He lived there in total silence for two months, eating wild berries, catching fish occasionally, but mostly fasting, meditating, waiting for instructions. One afternoon two local ladies from Taos stumbled upon him, brought him some food and meditated with him. Pretty soon rumor spread that a powerful being was living in the hills. People gathered from all over just to be in his presence. To meditate. To breathe as he breathed. They built him a small temple out of adobe, but he just laughed, preferring the cave. One evening, after doing an hour of connected breathing with one hundred of his ''followers,'' one person asked a question. Since no one had ever said a word to George, much less asked him a question, there was considerable interest in how he would respond, if at all.

"What is the truth?" was the question.

George thought about it for several minutes, laughing occasionally, which caused a ripple effect through the group. Finally, he said, "The truth is, there is no truth." The group buzzed. They would discuss this answer, debate and interpret it for years to come, but George would not be there to participate or elucidate. Because the next morning he packed his bags, climbed in his BMW and drove off.

Martha could have stayed at Tassajara forever. Meditation, chanting, karma yoga, good macrobiotic cooking. The routine fed her soul at its core, and she fell into a rhythm so easy, so smooth and so gentle her life became one endless, delicate, crystal clear flow, as constant as the fresh stream that rippled by the monastery. And those Tibetan bells. Whenever they chimed, they resonated throughout her body. So when she woke up one morning, after three months of bliss, and heard a voice in her head say, "Move on!," no one was more astonished than she was. When she asked herself why she was leaving, the voice said, "Why not?"

George parked at the Albuquerque airport and boarded a flight to Heathrow in London. He checked in at the Dorchester, bought two new tweed suits at Harrods, took high teas, and went to ten plays in eight days. He spent the rest of his time at pubs, drinking lager and lime, doing crossword puzzles. One night he was at the White Rabbit in Chelsea when a beautiful blonde walked in who reminded him of Martha. He broke into tears and buried his head on the bar. All his feelings trickled through him as, for the first time, he realized he might never see her again.

Martha was also crying as she floored the accelerator. She was heading east on Route 80, thinking about George, remembering his joke about the Jewish American Princess who indicates her orgasms by dropping her emery boards. It made her cry to think of all the times they laughed together. Then it made her laugh to think of all the times they cried together. And then it made her cry again to think of all the times they would not share together any more. She pulled into a gas station to recover herself and a teenage boy appeared at her window and asked, "How can I help you?"

"You can't," she said, and drove off into the dust.

George flew to Paris and stayed at a small hotel on the Left Bank. He stocked up on bread and cheese and a couple of bottles of Pouilly Fuisse, and hung out in his room for five days. He wrote a song for Martha,

> *Since you have left*
> *You've been with me all the time;*
> *Since you've been gone,*
> *I can't get you out of my mind.*
>
> *Will I ever see you again?*
> *I really don't know.*
> *I'll always be your friend*
> *Wherever I go.*

When he finally went out, he walked to Notre Dame, and when he entered, the awesome sanctity of the space drew silent tears from his heart. He climbed up to the tower, and when he saw the big old bell, he was reminded of her once again.

She couldn't get him out of her mind. She judged herself for holding on to him, thought she was doing this process all wrong, and finally she did what she had learned to do when she was completely stuck. She let go of her whole mind all at once. Her body was driving the car, but she was somewhere else. Walking on a cloud sprinkled with gold dust. As she walked on air, a figure approached from the distance. It was her father smoking his cigar.

"Where were you?" Alex asked.

"Nowhere."

"Well, now you're with me."

"Are you sure?"

"Where's George?"

"Someplace else."

"You kids, you do things different nowadays."

Martha came into her body with a thud. She had parked in the long-term lot at LAX. She put on her backpack, entered the international terminal and chose a flight to Tel Aviv. On the plane she slept soundly and didn't remember any dreams.

She rented a car and drove to Jerusalem, where she registered at the Hilton, then went to the Dome of the Rock and the Church of the Holy Sepulchre, where she had a vision of Mary and the baby Jesus, Orion and herself, all enjoying a picnic in the manger. Mary was telling her something she needed to know but didn't understand, something about how you can't leave your future behind you. . . .

George flew back to London, Martha to Paris. They actually crossed paths at Charles de Gaulle airport, but they didn't see each other.

George hired a limo at Gatwick and drove up to Glastonbury. He stayed at a bed and breakfast inn, and visited King Arthur's stomping grounds.

Martha hated Paris. She remembered all George's criticisms of the French, especially his comment about their being so full of themselves they had no room for anyone else. As soon as a taxi driver refused to speak French with her because of her American accent, which was minimal, she told him to drive her back to the airport. She'd try someplace else.

The day George went to the Tor it was so foggy he couldn't see his own feet. The Tor itself was a sacred spot, an old Druid ceremonial ground. He climbed up the ancient hill and stood on the top, a damp wind slapping his face and tossing his hair. It seemed to him that the entire hill was a ghost, that Arthurian legend was alive and well, if a bit invisible to the modern eye, in the mists of Avalon. George felt drawn to the place, and returned to the Tor every day for a week. The fog never lifted. He never saw the view. But he heard Gregorian chants in his head so loud and clear he knew he had crossed over into timelessness.

He went to the Tor one last time. He closed his eyes, breathed the biting air, and listened to the music in his mind. He was jolted by a body bumping into him, and when he looked up, a woman was turning towards him. He thought he recognized her way of turning. Déjà vu. She was so close but embraced by the mist. Then, suddenly, he saw who she was.

"Fancy meeting you here," she said.

Way #50: Breaking Up Is Hard to Do

If your purpose is to be together, so it will be. You cannot avoid your destiny, and your destiny is what you have freely chosen from the core of your soul. Once you have chosen, the end is inevitable. Only the means are up in the air. You can run away, divert your path, delay your destination, but in the end, you will find yourself where you were meant to be all along. It may take you by surprise when you get there. It may look completely different from your expectation, and feel totally unfamiliar. But you are going where you are going and with whom you have chosen to go. So relax and enjoy the ride.

And don't worry about loss. You can never lose what suits your higher purpose. If someone leaves you, it is to make room for someone better. Or if he is that someone better, he will return at the appropriate, even appointed time.

In the final analsyis, you are free to leave whenever you want. On the other hand, you can never leave what you have chosen to be with forever.

Affirmations

1. I'm free to leave.
2. My partner is free to leave.
3. My purpose is inevitable.
4. I never lose what's in my best interest.
5. Whatever belongs with me comes to me.
6. The more space we give each other, the clearer our purpose becomes.
7. The more space we give each other, the closer we grow.
8. Our love is not limited by time or space.
9. Our love is endless.
10. Our love always goes with us.
11. We are together even when we're apart.
12. I'm safe enough to release my fear of loss.
13. Since we are inseparable, we can be apart.
14. It's okay to get away from each other.
15. Being apart is not being separate.
16. When we're true to ourselves, we're true to each other.
17. Our individual quests support our joint purpose.
18. My personal desires support my relationship's purpose.
19. The more I follow my intuition, the more we grow.
20. When I leave my leaving pattern, I'm free.

OTHER BOOKS BY BOB MANDEL

from CELESTIAL ARTS PUBLISHING:
　　Open Heart Therapy
　　Two Hearts Are Better Than One
　　Birth and Relationships (co-authored with Sondra Ray)

from OPEN HEART PRODUCTIONS:
　　Money Mantras

and the following tapes (also from OPEN HEART PRODUCTIONS):
　　"Money Mantras"
　　"Having It All"
　　"Amazing You!"
　　"Peace With Passion"
　　"God Provides"

For information about rebirthing and the Loving Relationships Training, call 1-800-INTL-LRT, or write,
　　LRT International
　　P.O. Box 1465
　　Washington, CT 06793